The Entrepreneur Advantage

Emotional Intelligence for Building and Growing Your Business

ELIZABETH MINER

Patagonia ad used with permission: "Don't Buy This Jacket" by Tim Nudd, November 25, 2011, New York Times

EPUB: ISBN: 978-1-7373800-0-9
PDF ISBN: 978-1-7373800-1-6
Mobi ISBN: 978-1-7373800-2-3
ePIB ISBN: 978-1-7373800-3-0
Paperback ISBN: 978-1-7373800-4-7

Editing by: Steve Arensberg

Book design by: Paper Lime Creative

A Publication Offered by

Thrive This Day
210 Park Avenue #900
Worcester, MA 01609

www.ElizabethMiner.net

Dedicated to those building visions
from what others have not yet seen.

Table of Contents

Foreword

I'd just closed my DREAM client.

It'd taken a while, but I finally closed the deal I envisioned when I started as an entrepreneur. It had all the characteristics of my ideal client — the ones listed on a piece of paper taped above my desk. This paper had been there for what seemed like forever, and it was exhilarating to have this dream finally come to fruition.

It was happening, and I was happy and on top of the world! This was what being an entrepreneur was all about, right?

Then a global pandemic hit, and my dream client vanished overnight. I felt angry.

The night after I got the news about my client, I overheard some of my friends bragging about how much they were killing it in their companies… steady paychecks and big bonuses!

Truly "salt in the wound."

I spent days feeling hopeless and demoralized. Is the entrepreneur life really for me?

Slowly, I emerged from the fog of disappointment and began to think through how I would pivot.

Fortunately, I was able to pick up the pieces and discovered an unexpected path forward that led to my biggest and best year for my company.

This experience is just one example of the emotional roller coaster and brutality of life as an entrepreneur. The entrepreneurial journey can be punishing and leave you dreaming of your friend's stable paycheck and bonus.

Although I went to business school and had various mentors, none of that prepared me for the extreme ups and downs. The harsh reality is this: a business plan, clarity on your dream client, and passion aren't enough to achieve success. Even landing your dream client isn't enough.

One of the keys is to remind yourself why you began your path as an entrepreneur. It can offer a light to guide you. For me, it's freedom, aliveness, and the opportunity... to fully use my strengths and passion to pursue a richer life and potential bigger financial upside... right around the corner.

There's an element missing in most entrepreneurship training, which tends to focus only on the product or the client or the marketing. That missing element is understanding the "human engine of the business," as my friend, Elizabeth Miner, calls it. That's *you*, entrepreneur.

I met Elizabeth years ago at a conference in Portland, Oregon. We instantly hit it off as we were both early in our entrepreneur journeys then. We both recognized that mastering the mental side of entrepreneurship is the hardest, and yet the least addressed.

That's where Elizabeth comes in. She felt called to write a book to help entrepreneurs conquer this difficult aspect of the journey. She's channeled her experience as an endurance athlete and her amazing work with clients into a powerful message that gives entrepreneurs an advantage.

As she says, it's important to consider your life as an entrepreneur as a "marathon and not a sprint."

I agree, and this is easier said than done. See my personal story above! I can't say if I'd had Elizabeth's book that I'd have avoided all of the challenges that came my way (pandemic, anyone?) but I can say it's likely that I'd have had more tools to better deal with those challenges — physical, mental, emotional — I've faced in my years as an entrepreneur.

With the skills Elizabeth teaches in this book, you too can learn to keep your "why" in front of you as a beacon (chapter 3). You will learn to prepare mind and body for the hardships that will undoubtedly come — whether a lost client, a personal challenge, or even a pandemic (chapters 4 and 11). You will learn when to pivot (or pitch), and how you make those difficult decisions at your best (chapter 6).

And, perhaps most of all, you will learn about yourself, and what it takes for you to endure in your own entrepreneurial race.

I'm delighted to have this book as a guide to address the mental side of this sometimes-difficult journey and create my own entrepreneur advantage. I think you will too.

–Ben Fanning
#1 bestselling author and
host of *The CEO Sessions* podcast

The Entrepreneur Marathon

Standing in a sea of people, you feel a potent mix of excitement, anxiety, courage, pride, and fear flowing through your body. Everyone around you is just like you: they have prepared for this moment for months, maybe even thought about it for years. Each person is there with the same goal in mind, yet alone in their individual pursuit.

"HONKKKKKK!" The starting horn sounds.

You and hundreds of others take your first steps in the long race ahead. You've planned for this and you feel ready — yet you are still anxious about what lies before you. You know no matter how well you know the course, the hills, the terrain, the checkpoints, and your own ability, there is so much that might derail you, no matter how well you've trained.

It feels like an eternity as you watch so many start ahead of you while you patiently wait your turn. Finally, you arrive at the start line and cross it, stepping onto the course buoyed by the sound of cheers from the small crowd gathered to see you off.

This is the moment you've waited for. You've spent months preparing — in stolen moments in the early mornings before the rest of your day began, or late nights after you completed your other commitments. You carved out the time to work for this.

Although you put in the time and effort to get here, you know very well that all that work, though necessary, does not guarantee the reward at the end. How you perform once you cross that starting line is what determines your results or if you even reach your goal at all.

Training Body and Mind

Endurance athletes understand that there are two important parts of training. One is conditioning the body to go the distance. The other is training the mind as it controls everything.

Early into the course the mind games begin. Did you go out too fast? Will you have enough energy to go the distance? Did you bring enough fuel? Where are your people? They said they'd be here!

Further in, fears creep up, as do voices of pessimism and doubt, the whiny child, and the "are we there yet?" mantra. Training mindset ahead of time prepares you to deal with each of these (and more) thoughts and voices that will come up throughout the course.

Understanding where each of these thoughts comes from, what prompts them, and what they mean to you is important. This way, you know when they will arise and how to deal with them best.

As you move along the course you notice the field narrowing; there are fewer people at your pace. You see some people slow to a walk; some even leave the course. You realize you have more miles behind you than those that lie ahead. You've come so far that quitting now would be such a tough call... but the thought runs through your mind from time to time.

When you arrive at mile 18 and you feel that burn in your legs, how you assess it and manage your emotions can be the difference between hurting yourself and finishing what you came to accomplish. Do you just "Suck it up, buttercup," or do you slow down and walk it out? Do you use the aid station when you feel the pain, or do you run past the tent designed to assist those in need? Do you stop to avoid risking injury, or is what you're feeling something you can work through?

Any endurance athlete will tell you the thoughts that come to them during an event are deeper and more prevalent than any other time. When the stakes are high, adrenaline surges, and pride is on the line, the thoughts and voices get louder. Knowing this and how to deal with it is what helps the athlete prepare for and perform their best.

Having a plan for the thoughts, concerns, and behaviors that will show up at the most inconvenient time will make sure they do not derail the race you've come to run. Understanding how you evaluate your present state, knowing what you've set out to do and why, and knowing what the accomplishment means to you will allow you to survive a DNF (did not finish) and learn a lesson to make you better for your next event.

When you finally reach the end of the course, you see the glorious finish line and hear the cheering crowds. Maybe you bask in the glory of your accomplishment. Maybe those numbers above the finish line speak to you — offering pride or disappointment. You must prepare for this, too — because the end of this course is often just the start of a new one.

The Entrepreneurial Starting Line

It is often said that being an entrepreneur is a marathon and not a sprint. I couldn't agree more. As a marathoner and an entrepreneur, I can easily draw comparisons between the two.

Like endurance training, the operational aspects of entrepreneurship are only half the equation. Unfortunately, most entrepreneurship training misses the mindset portion. Current entrepreneurial education is like only conditioning the body, and in the endurance game, mindset is essential. It's no wonder that those who don't train their minds to go the entrepreneurial distance often don't reach the success they wish — they've only done half the training.

Leaving mindset to chance increases the odds that you will become part of the statistics who don't go the distance. Your state of mind plays a part in so many elements of a successful business that ignoring this piece before you set out is a recipe for a disappointing finish at best — or a DNF at worst.

Every time a marathoner laces up for a course, they know there's no guarantee they'll run their best race. Being prepared — both physically and mentally — is how they thrive through the challenge each course presents.

This book will guide you as you embark on the second part of your training: conditioning the mind of the entrepreneur.

CHAPTER 1

Why Businesses Fail, and How Not To

Whenever you start a new business, the sheer number of variables at hand makes failure a constant possibility.
–Sally Krawcheck

Why Businesses Fail

When you talk about starting a business, the first comment you hear is the failure rate. **Just over half of businesses survive their first five years.**

What the statistics don't tell you is *why* businesses fail. There is a story behind the numbers — and human behavior is tied to each of them.

Business schools will teach you about business metrics, operational strategy, and industry expectations, but they rarely dive into the one common factor in all businesses: they are all run by humans (at least today!).

This critical and often overlooked human element is why this book exists. In these pages, we'll dive into the psyche (mindset) of an entrepreneur, to reveal what drives behavior and decisions. This knowledge can make all the difference between failure and success.

My sister used to say, "Humans are emotional, and emotions are irrational; therefore, humans are irrational." It is a simplistic mathematical equation, and though not completely true, it's a good place to start.

Human behavior is not logic-based; if it were, we would all be like the character Spock on *Star Trek*. Most of us believe we use logic and sound reasoning to make decisions and behave in a manner consistent with that. But really, few of us think like Spock at all.

Even when logic is active, the behavior of us mere earthlings — entrepreneurs included — originates with emotions. Knowing the effects of our emotions on our behaviors is where the power lies.

As I've worked with entrepreneurs over many years, I have come to understand that although it is true humans are emotional and emotion drives behavior, humans can also be quite predictable. Understanding emotions — our own and those of others — can help us understand and even avoid the irrational part of the equation.

The more you understand the emotional impact driving your behaviors and decisions, the better you can notice conflicting elements, and course correct.

What Exactly Is Emotional Intelligence?

Emotional intelligence, also known as emotional quotient (EQ), is "the capacity to be aware of, control, and express one's emotions." (Oxford Languages) Your level of EQ informs much of the way you think and behave, and how you react and interact with others.

EQ includes how you view the world, your place in it, and your relationship to others around you. It includes your ability to recognize, understand, and manage emotions, and encompasses self-awareness, self-regulation, motivation, empathy, and social skills.

For some of you, EQ might sound a bit too theoretical, or too "woo-woo" for serious business. But think of it this way: businesses are built on thousands of decisions, big and small. And as much as we'd like it to be different, our behavior and decisions are more emotional than logical. Therefore, your emotional state and how you arrived there is of major importance to making the most effective decisions in and for your business.

Some of you may already see how developing and enhancing emotional intelligence can have a positive effect on your business. In this book, we'll break down each of these elements so you can uncover and fully grasp how each might drive behavior and ultimately your success.

As you understand your emotions and those of your team, clients, and even vendors, you will make better decisions, be a better leader, and have a stronger business overall. Your EQ is relevant in every phase and stage of your business — having a good understanding from the inception of your business will hold significant benefits for you.

Consider this book the owner's manual for the most important part of your business: you. When you finish this book, you'll have the tools and knowledge to face the challenges and ups and downs that come with being an entrepreneur, and you'll have the greatest chance for success because you have given yourself this advantage.

Who Is an Entrepreneur?

The term entrepreneur has a wide-ranging definition depending on whom you ask. Entrepreneurs are the Mark Zuckerburgs and Steve Jobs of the world, and the mom-and-pop shop down the street. They are the corporate conglomerates founded in somebody's garage, or your best friend running a home-based business on the side — and everything in between.

What these entrepreneurs have in common is this: how they see themselves (their role) in the world, how they think, and how they make decisions all affect the businesses they run — regardless of size, industry, or location.

EQ for Entrepreneurs

Your life and business integrate, no matter how good your boundaries are. You are the one human in both areas of your life. It is impossible for your experiences in one realm of your life not to affect every other area.

Since you will carry your life experiences into your business, you benefit from understanding how they may show up and what to do with them when they do. Having a solid understanding of the human engine driving the business machine can be a distinct advantage, but it requires thoughtful introspection and management.

My years as a life coach have revealed how much people's experiences affect their daily choices and decisions. In my work with entrepreneurs, I saw the same pattern repeating in their businesses and their personal lives, often in major — but also avoidable — ways.

Their mindset, personal history, and emotional understanding and control — every aspect of their EQ — affected how they did everything: from how they made the simplest decisions, to how they led their teams, to how they protected against burnout — or succumbed to it. EQ ultimately was a critical element to their success, stress level, and effectiveness as a leader in business.

Think about this:

You step into a room filled with venture capitalists with pads of paper and laptops in front of them. They turn to see who walked through the door; you feel every eye in the room on you.

You're about to make the presentation of your life. You've prepared for this, staying up late, reworking the slide deck, going over your numbers, making sure everything is as good as it can be. You feel confident — or at least you did a minute ago!

Suddenly, the time when you did your first book report in third grade comes to mind, or the struggles you watched your family go through as a kid.

Or maybe in a flash you replay last night's discussion with your partner and the worry they expressed about going into debt. Or your own fears creep in — about not having enough money to build your business and pay your bills.

Whatever goes through your mind in this moment is going to affect how you deliver this presentation. It will affect your confidence, and how you interpret the expressions (or lack of) from your audience. It will affect who you look at during the presentation, which figures or data you present, and how you answer their questions.

This is not a fictional story; it is a real-life example of what happens every day to entrepreneurs. They prepare all the charts, strategy, and figures for their business, but they often neglect to prepare *themselves*.

There are so many times where your life and business will intersect; I've seen it happen over and over again. Will you use that intersection to your advantage, or let it take advantage of you?

Learning how your experiences and emotions show up in your entrepreneurial life will not prevent them from showing up, but it will prepare you for if, how, and when they may appear and how best to manage them when they do.

EQ for You

In your quest to be the entrepreneur who is successful against the odds and statistics, developing your EQ is imperative. This requires insight and awareness as a foundation.

Once you understand your personal EQ, the question becomes how to make it work to your advantage. In each chapter, we'll explore the critical areas of emotional intelligence for you to learn and apply, how and where they show up in business, and how to develop them for your advantage. This is not therapy; you are building awareness and tactics to make the most of who you are, and to recognize where and how to supplement who you are not.

What you learn about yourself and those around you will put you in the driver's seat with a clear road map for your success.

CHAPTER 2

The Life Cycle of the Entrepreneur

In this chapter:
- Reality-check our beliefs about entrepreneurship.
- Review the four stages of the entrepreneur life cycle and how EQ relates.

Creating a business out of nothing more than an idea is a mix of parenting and an endurance sport — on a roller-coaster ride — all playing out in public view.

I don't say this to scare you (okay, maybe a little!), but to inform you of the ride you are about to embark on or already have found yourself on. Knowing what's ahead will help you prepare. Although the pace of the ride will vary, you can count on the stages being similar.

This is a book about the emotional intelligence required to become a successful entrepreneur, which doesn't happen overnight. I designed this book to help you develop awareness and skills over time as you and your business evolve.

No matter the size of the business, the entrepreneurial path requires we develop the same emotional awareness, capabilities, and fortitude to be successful.

Understanding the requirements for succeeding as an entrepreneur — at each stage of your company's life cycle — is as important to the success of your business as the offering itself.

We've seen too many great companies and ideas mismanaged by those who didn't have the emotional intelligence to lead well. We've seen too many opportunities lost by those not equipped to adjust to the changing needs of their company or the market. And we've seen too many companies attempting to hold on to what they know, fearing change, and losing sight of the needs of their customers.

You are here to avoid the mistakes that create those failure rate statistics for entrepreneurs. I am here to help you prepare for the adventure you are about to embark on, no matter in what phase of business you find yourself today or in the future.

Before We Begin: A Reality Check

Let's look at what entrepreneurship's initial stages require.

When a rocket ship launches into space, it burns approximately 31% of its resources or fuel to accomplish liftoff alone. New entrepreneurial ventures are similar. There is so much needed at the initial stages of building a business: clarifying the vision, generating engagement, and attracting clients, customers, and potential partners.

Most people anticipate the number of hours they will need to spend and maybe even the energy. But many don't really understand the drain this has on a person. As much as we don't like to admit it — especially we entrepreneurs — we are human and have limitations.

I could parrot others and tell you to just hustle and work harder and more than anyone else. I disagree that what you need to get through this stage is endless grit, countless hours, and some energy bars and drinks. That's "Bull" without the "Red"!

The 'hustle' culture is a recipe for burnout, self-harm, and neglect of yourself and others you love. It will not bring out your best and is not sustainable for the duration needed.

On the flip side is the claim that you can build a successful empire in a minimal amount of hours, as long as you achieve maximum productivity. While this may be true for some businesses, for most it is not. This model requires the ability to have distraction-free time, resources, and systems that most early stage entrepreneurs do not have.

Let's face it — as an entrepreneur in a new venture or business, you cannot exist in a world without distraction! You can have pockets of focused time without interruption, but you must plan and schedule them so others can predict your availability.

As the master of the vision and the generator of the idea, you will be a necessary point of contact for anyone assisting or desiring what you are bringing to market. You will require more than four hours a week in almost every case. And trust me when I say this: working on the beach is not as great as it looks. (I know, I've tried!)

Taking a concept from idea to reality is a complex process that transforms along the course. The person at the helm of this process must recognize and adapt to the requirements of each phase of development.

Phase 1: The Big Bang

It all starts with an idea and the desire to bring that idea to reality.

The beginning stages of entrepreneurship are where you are building momentum and navigating through the initial rough patches with enthusiasm and excitement. This requires the energy to move forward when few others see the vision you have.

Having confidence in your abilities, knowing why you are willing to forge through the challenges of creating a business, and being fully aware of your strengths and weaknesses are all qualities you will need during this time more than any other.

You must continually show up and move your idea from your head into the real world. To succeed in this, you must hone your communication skills and your ability to step outside yourself.

As you move through this stage, you will need more than excitement as your idea encounters the real world. Your enthusiasm may flag, and impatience may set in. Some days will be great; some, not so much. It's all part of the process.

A key ingredient for this stage is self-motivation, fueled at the beginning by the excitement you feel for your idea. Self-awareness will be the foundation for how you handle everything you encounter at this stage and in every other throughout your journey.

Phase 2: Evolution

As you move into the "adolescent stage" of building your business, you will need devotion, much like a parent. During those days when you face resistance, you may need to reach into your memory to remember the excitement and love you hold for the idea. You may have days you feel like no matter what you do, you're getting things wrong. You will need to keep pushing forward during these times, which requires steadfastness and tenacity.

There is so much changing and developing during this phase of the journey. You may feel the need to adjust your idea to better meet the needs of your prospective clients or customers. You may identify unexpected costs or needs you've not budgeted for.

You must understand how you manage change and decision-making so these circumstances don't derail you. As an entrepreneur you can expect the unexpected, and you must prepare yourself to manage the stress and emotional strain of these times.

Phase 3: Plateau

Continuing to move through the process — especially when the journey to reach the destination you desired is longer than you initially expected — is a form of endurance. Much like a marathon runner or any type of extreme athlete, these times will test your grit. The ability to push forward when you feel you should already be "there" requires a mindset trained to forgo the attachment of time and remain focused on the desired result.

If you haven't yet connected with a mentor or a mastermind group, you will benefit by having others you can talk with during this phase. Knowing when you need support and having trusted advisors (not intimately connected to you) is an important part of staying on your best course.

During this stage, you will encounter a new set of emotional strains, stresses, and different levels of decisions. You may find yourself at a stage of your business where many waver in their commitment or question the value of what they are doing. It's important to understand what support is available to you and how to connect with your trusted sources for guidance and advice.

Phase 4: Graduation

After you have "arrived," you must begin maintaining what you've built. As Simon Sinek states in his book, *The Infinite Game,* "There is no end goal to be achieved in the continued of pursuit of your 'just cause.'" Unlike an endurance athlete, there is no finish line for the successful entrepreneur, only a new start line.

The ability to enjoy and build on your initial success creates a whole new set of questions to answer, decisions to make, and skills to develop. How you move forward when you've reached your initial goal is not a forgone conclusion. You have many options at this stage, and self-awareness will remain the foundation of your best decision.

Each Stage Requires Emotional Intelligence

The emotional life cycle for an entrepreneur differs from the operational life cycle of a business. Inextricably connected, each cannot survive without the best understanding of the other.

Knowing what you need at each stage and having the awareness about yourself puts you in the position to succeed not only in business but also in other areas of your life at the same time. As an emotionally intelligent entrepreneur, you bring a solid base on which to build your business — which benefits the business, its growth, and the clients and customers it serves.

Part 1

Foundations of the Entrepreneur Self

CHAPTER 3

Self-Awareness

Man is affected not by events, but by the view he takes of them.
-Epictetus

In this chapter:
- Explore weaknesses and strengths.
- Recognize where life experiences may intersect with business.
- Develop methods to address the impact of experiences.

Self-awareness is the most important skill to develop as an entrepreneur. Knowing oneself fully and being aware of the driving force behind the actions you take will enable you to direct or redirect your strengths and weaknesses, your beliefs and biases. This is the primary foundation for building a strong EQ.

Once you know how you react in certain circumstances — those reflexive reactions to situations — you open a veritable map to how to navigate your world. In business, self-awareness can be the difference between costly poor decisions or strategic alignment during crisis.

Take Richard Branson, arguably one of the most successful entrepreneurs of today. Knowing himself has allowed him to capitalize on his skills and support his weaknesses to manage business challenges — and create and develop hundreds of companies.

Having solid self-awareness has enabled him to make strategic decisions aligned to his vision, and having a sound bearing on his emotions, risk tolerance, and values has allowed him to walk away from business ideas that were not a match for him or his brand.

An entrepreneur's emotions, reactions, and bias are important to every element of their business. Failing to be aware and manage these things can blindside the entrepreneur in a critical phase — or even destroy a business over time.

The mindset of an entrepreneur holds tremendous influence in creating the culture of the business, the talent it attracts, and the overall personality of the company. Because so much rests on the entrepreneur, even beyond the creation of the product or service, there is further education needed in this subject before stepping into the arena.

This Is Not a Test

It is not enough to take a test or two that tells you your personality type or propensity for a style of leadership. To be self-aware is not just having a set of labels that defines you; it is recognizing the basis for your viewpoints, sensitivities, and strengths.

Entrepreneurs are humans filled with experiences that shape the way they view the world. These experiences can create positive or negative associations to situations that are commonplace in business. Knowing the framework through which you view circumstances is tremendously helpful.

Entrepreneurs often skip this first important step because self-awareness does not appear to speak to their product or the work of creating it. And to be honest, it's hard. But skipping this part is ultimately detrimental to the success of your enterprise, because self-awareness is the foundation for your greatest success.

Self-awareness is the key component in the operating system for the human. As an entrepreneur, you are the source of everything your business is and will become. Your product or service is important, yes, but no matter how amazing your offering is, your operating system will affect everything, from the initial product creation, to sales, to delivery, to customer service.

Clear self-awareness gives you the guidance to put to use all the benefits of your personal operating system and address any bugs that might impede progress — or worse, crash the system.

The Foundation of Your Business

Consider self-awareness like the foundation of a building. When constructing a building, a critical part is designing the foundation and knowing the requirements to support what you wish to build upon it. From there you'll know exactly how much weight, the approximate size, material, and structure you can place upon it.

Overlook this important assessment and you could end up with a structure that will collapse under the weight. Or you might overbuild the structure and waste resources.

The next consideration is your building's environment. What types of storms or other extreme elements will your building need to weather? How long are the seasons and how should you design for those extremes?

You wouldn't build a skyscraper — or even a shed — without considering this information. Don't build your business without it, either. Knowing the real load-bearing weight of the entrepreneur — and how a company on this foundation will withstand and react to the expected elements — is the foundational self-awareness we will examine in this chapter.

There is so much to consider when doing a full self-assessment, which is why this is the critical beginning of your journey. If you get no further than completing this chapter, you will reap tremendous benefits. (But don't stop here, there is much more to come!)

The Founder

This book is not about making you the perfect business founder or having the perfect business. It is not about eliminating flaws, biases, or personal tendencies. This book will help you develop an understanding of each aspect of yourself and recognize what you might need to produce the best results for your business.

In this section, we'll cover two important areas of self-awareness: personal history, which shapes your perspectives, biases, and tendencies; and strengths and weaknesses — those natural facilities or struggles that shape your approaches.

Personal History

We are each a product of our experiences. This shows up in everything we think and do, which has an incredible impact on how each entrepreneur manages their company. Nowhere is self-awareness more important than in knowing the stories an entrepreneur carries with them.

Each occurrence in life leaves an impression on the brain, as reference material for the future. For us humans, an experience does not stand alone; we assign meaning (whether true or not) to each impression, which we use in the future.

These impressions and meanings become biases and assumptions that knowingly or unknowingly influence decisions and behaviors. As an entrepreneur, being aware of experiences and how they might affect consideration in business will be essential for success. We will address decision-making in greater depth in chapter 6.

A clear understanding of how our past plays into our behaviors, risk profile, and emotional state helps us decide action plans best suited for any situation. This is a process that will continue to reveal itself throughout the entrepreneurial journey, but I recommend thinking about it early and often.

Our experiences continually influence our daily decisions, which can be a good thing. Experiences can prevent repeat mistakes. However, they can also sway decisions — either compensating for past failures or responding to something from our personal history.

Entrepreneurs are best served when they have a clear awareness of what drives their thoughts in any situation. Through this understanding, entrepreneurs can use or defuse experiences and thoughts and create a beneficial outcome.

No matter your past, understanding how your experiences play into your mindset will provide you with the ability to manage the effect beneficially.

Strengths and Weaknesses

Most job interviews include questions about strengths and weaknesses. Knowing these answers is just as important to you as an entrepreneur.

The difficulty is that as an entrepreneur no one is asking you this question — you must ask it of yourself and address the answers accordingly. Once you understand your strengths and weaknesses, you can apply the information to each area of your business as needed.

The first step is to acknowledge your strengths and weaknesses. Then you will have the ability to move within them. This is where self-assessment pays off: there are countless methods to help you shore up or work with weaknesses, and you can only apply them if you're aware of your individual weaknesses.

Denying a weakness has no benefit and can be harmful to the overall business. Once you realize that having weaknesses is not bad, you'll move through this process much faster.

Beware of blind spots here. Reach out to others who know you for feedback to give yourself the most accurate picture. This is a space to celebrate — because once you know your areas of weakness, you can address them.

I Know My Weaknesses — Now What?

There are many ways to deal with your weaknesses. I am a firm believer that taking time to create strengths out of weaknesses is not a good use of this precious resource. In some cases you might find it necessary, if only for a time; in most, however, you're better off approaching your weaknesses differently.

Delegation is a highly effective option for entrepreneurs to remove tasks in their areas of weakness. This allows the entrepreneur to concentrate where they can make the most impact while they ensure all tasks are managed. Delegation is an underutilized tool for most of us, and the entrepreneur will benefit by using this tool in both personal and professional arenas.

Creating systems is another method to manage some weaknesses. Many technological tools on the market today can help you manage everything from customers to task lists. For every entrepreneur with a weakness, another entrepreneur has faced it, solved it for themselves, and brought the solution to market.

With a clear understanding of the areas where you need support, creating systems is a great way to manage weaknesses. Use routines, tools (either paper or electronic), or other structures. The most important part of working with systems is finding the right fit for you.

Be certain that using a system actually saves time, minimizes points of failure, or maximizes productivity. Don't allow a system to require more effort than it saves and be alert to putting a system into place that adds distractions. As an entrepreneur, you don't need more distractions!

Recognizing your weaknesses can be difficult. Often, it requires unflinching honesty with yourself, about topics you've avoided or hidden for many years. None of us like to be shown our weaknesses or flaws and judged for them (whether others truly judge us, or it just feels that way). No human being wants criticism or rejection, so we downplay, ignore, or avoid those areas of weakness. This avoidance behavior can, over time, render our weaknesses almost invisible.

The same is often true of one's strengths. Because the way we act is so ingrained in us, we don't recognize it as unique. We can easily be blind to our natural tendencies because for us they are... well... just natural.

For example, if you are really a creative thinker, you might not even notice how you approach issues differently than others do. You may come up with a unique answer or you might really enjoy problem solving because it allows your creativity to come out. But you might not even recognize this as a strength because that is just the way you are.

Or if you are a very detail-oriented person, you may not realize it — because noticing details is just the way you see life. You may catch the missing item or notice the smallest changes that others overlook.

It is likely something so natural to you that you don't even recognize it as a potential strength.

When I work with clients, I often ask them to get input from people close to them for honest feedback on both strengths and weaknesses.

Mind the Gap

As an entrepreneur, it is up to you to set your goals and deliver on them. This needs to be a constant practice long before you have clients or customers. Before you can keep promises to others, you must learn to deliver on your promises to yourself.

While considering strengths and weaknesses, please do not fall for the lie that as an entrepreneur you must "be all things to your business at all times." This cannot be further from the truth – and the moment you realize this lie, you'll relieve yourself of some pressure.

Knowing where gaps exist between your needs and your weaknesses is one of the greatest gifts of self-awareness. Once you understand what areas you need to enhance, you can address those needs in the best way available to you.

Motivation

At the very beginning of entrepreneurship, when an idea is fresh and new, excitement and motivation are easy. Even when there are so many things before you, it's likely the idea or business itself has encountered little resistance like rejection and obstacles simply by its age and exposure.

Once you get past your own limiting beliefs and the few you may encounter as you share your project, most entrepreneurs are focused and hopeful, which is why they begin their business in the first place. This is a time of great momentum and it is easier to spring out of bed each morning with anticipation of bringing this great idea to light.

Entrepreneurship is all about endurance though and motivation isn't an endurance sport. Babe Ruth was right when he said, "It's hard to beat a person who never gives up."

Motivation does not precede action; action drives motivation. The daily work required to succeed is sometimes daunting, and in those moments, self-discipline will pull you through.

One way to spark motivation is to review your personal and professional goals. There is a definite energy and clarity that comes from this practice and yes, I recommend it as a daily practice.

Reviewing the goals you set puts you in the mindset of what you are trying to accomplish through your business. By doing this activity daily, you are continually renewing your commitment to do the work necessary. This is also a great way to infuse energy into your business. Sometimes the mundane task checking off and the magnitude of a project brings us so far away from our goals. A reminder of why you are putting forth this energy and what great things will come from the work will be beneficial.

The Stories We Create

Self-awareness goes much deeper than simply our strengths and weaknesses, however; we also need to be aware about how we come to conclusions. As a walking collection of experiences, we come to any new venture with a personal library that will affect our work.

Knowing what drives our thoughts is critical to determining if they are helpful or harmful. Once aware, we can take steps to mitigate any damage and make the clearest, best decisions for our business.

The category of self-awareness is huge, and it's easy to get overwhelmed analyzing the thought processes that affect each decision we make. Let's work with just a few with the strongest impact.

Ego

One area of exploration that has direct or immediate impact on entrepreneurship is ego.

You may or may not think you have an issue with ego, but it drives everyone. From the pleaser to the avoider, ego will play a role in work styles and behaviors. The sooner it becomes clear how ego shows up for you, the easier it will be to address and manage.

You'll gain perspective as you learn which of your beliefs are driven or even colored by your ego and past stories. The purpose of this knowledge is so you avoid making decisions only to overcome your experiences, but instead you decide based on present circumstances and facts.

The feeling of worthiness comes up for many of us when we begin our journey. Worthiness may not be obvious as such, but it is often there in some form. For some, the idea of becoming an entrepreneur and creating something of value is an opportunity to prove that they, as humans, are worthy. The thought of leaving a legacy is their contribution and proof of value during their time on the earth.

For some, pursuing financial gains as proof of value has a clear connection to ego and worthiness. This causes issues with both the insatiable drive for "enough" money, and the reaction and disproportionate impact of failure or losses.

Money usually carries meaning that is far deeper for these people, and this underlying meaning can influence judgment and leadership. Being aware of your thoughts and perspectives around money will allow you to navigate these feelings while running your business.

Superhero/Lone-Wolf Syndrome

Another area that is detrimental to success for some entrepreneurs is the belief that they must do everything themselves. The inability to delegate or the idea that no one other than the entrepreneur can do a task well enough is unhealthy, limiting, and a direct path to burnout.

"Nobody does things right!" Rose said. "I give projects to others and I always have to do clean-up work."

Rose had continually complained that she was working so many hours and needed to get a break. When the question of hiring others or delegating work came up, she protested, "I'll have to explain everything. I could have just done it myself by the time I get through explaining. And besides, no one gets it right on the first try!"

We talked about how she handles work that isn't done "to her standards." Rose said, "I just fix it. I don't have time to explain what they did wrong, because it's already taken too much time for me by that point."

"How will they improve if they don't know what they've done wrong?" I asked. "If you give them a chance to learn what they've done wrong, sure it will take longer... this time, but you won't have to correct the same error next time."

Sometimes an entrepreneur contributes to the problem of not being able to delegate by assuming others understand the expectations, or by not showing people where they have made mistakes to prevent them from happening again. In the harried environment of a new business, it pays off in the long run to put the time into building a team that can grow with the company.

An entrepreneur who has difficulty handing over or even loosening the reins on any part of the business will have trouble. This situation can be a simple trust issue or relate to something deeper and more personal. However this difficulty manifests, the entrepreneur must deal with it, for the immediate and ultimate good of their business.

This belief or leadership style is detrimental to both the entrepreneur and anyone they work with. This practice removes the opportunity for others to contribute and undermines the very skills and talents they offer, and limits the depth of a business by reducing diversity of perspective, and representing only one source of knowledge.

There are no bonus points for being a martyr in business. It takes courage to allow others to contribute to the final product of one's dream. When you allow others to take part, you open the possibility to expand and enhance the business at the same time sharing the workload to prevent overwhelm and burnout.

The Ongoing Process of Self-Awareness

There are so many aspects of knowing oneself — and we are continually evolving — so developing self-awareness is not a "one and done" process. Self-awareness is fluid and will continue to change as we do.

Self-awareness is more than determining your Myers-Briggs indicators or Enneagram type, although those are great to know. This goes deeper into identifying your behaviors, thought process, and experiences in different circumstances.

How a person approaches issues and the background of experiences and information they draw from will affect decisions, leadership, the culture of the business, and so much more. Having this self-knowledge and applying it is how an entrepreneur can leverage their great EQ.

For example: do you dislike confrontation or struggle with tough conversations? Are you intensely competitive? Maybe you are a perfectionist or struggle with being a people-pleaser? Any of these characteristics may show up in some aspect of your business and if they are positive or negative depends on how you use them.

Self-awareness is a continual process of questioning oneself and receiving feedback from others. This is an ongoing journey that will not only make you a better entrepreneur but also a better partner, family member, and friend. Understanding yourself and knowing how you operate touches every aspect of your life.

Sometimes a person's strongest qualities are their biggest downfalls if not managed well. Being brutally honest to understand character, strengths, and weaknesses is essential for you to create your best opportunity for success. We must be willing to explore honestly, knowing that anything we uncover will help us if put to proper use.

Time Well Spent, No Matter the Outcome

Andrea was a client of mine a few years ago. She had come to me with a great idea that she wanted to create a business around. We worked for several months together to understand the requirements to bring this idea forward and to put a plan together.

The closer we got to being ready to launch the idea, the more stress Andrea felt. She wrote it off as a normal product of launching a new business.

Finally, she couldn't take the pressure anymore and she called to discuss her feelings. "I don't think I really want to do this," she confessed. "I've wasted so much time!"

As we sorted out her thoughts, it turned out that at that time in her life she was not willing to take on the uncertainty of beginning her own business. After discussing her circumstances, the decision to pursue her own business seemed right for her when she began, but our working together had given her tremendous clarity and confidence in what she had to offer, and also in what she wanted (and didn't).

Andrea went on to work as an executive at a start-up, where she could not only use what she had learned from her own entrepreneurial experience but also ease the pressure on herself compared to building her own business from the ground up.

The self-awareness she developed in working through the goals and plans of starting a business gave her the insight to determine what was best for her in this current time.

Self-awareness will provide guidance, save unnecessary pain, create more diverse products and services, strengthen your leadership qualities all while benefiting your personal life. You cannot afford to begin your entrepreneurial journey without first taking stock of the foundation that everything in your company will depend on.

Make time for this important exploration and you will avoid being blindsided by your past and feel more in control when nothing else feels that way. Know where to seek help and what you are looking for in partners and others to fill your known gaps for the needs of your business, and you will increase productivity.

There are no benefits to you by naming something a good or bad trait; simply being aware is the goal. Once aware, you can maximize positive or minimize negative effects. This is when you will reap the rewards of your knowledge.

It is important to note that character and strengths are not set characteristics — we can develop or enhance them. Improvement takes cultivated awareness, desire, and time for growth, but it is ᷄ tirely possible. Some development will happen organically, and the rest will require effort. Knowing which modifications will make the most difference, and where, will help you determine where to focus.

Working on this first, crucial EQ ability will be continual — but you must start now. Understanding yourself is a key factor in how you run your business — from the minor tasks to the major decisions. Self-awareness about how you work, make decisions, and lead is critical for optimally running your business.

Get this started now and you are on your way.

Self-Awareness Exercises

Take a few minutes to journal on and think about each of the following questions.

Life-Influencing Experiences

- Think about your childhood and how your parents talked about work and what they did for careers. Consider how their fears or behaviors might have influenced you.

- Think about how you approached school and what you did in your childhood days. Were you a daredevil type of child or did you do everything "by the rules"? Did you embrace the freedom to try new things, or did failure make you feel unsafe?

- Is there any other experience you've had that might influence how you approach your business today?

Strengths and Weaknesses

- What is something that you simply cannot not do? What do people seek your advice or expertise on?

- What tasks or projects energize or excite you about being an entrepreneur?

- What tasks or projects do you hate or avoid as an entrepreneur?

- What resources can you explore to address some of your weaknesses?

Your Entrepreneurial Story

- Why have you chosen to become an entrepreneur? What drives your desire to build a business instead of working for someone else?

- What do you hope to gain by building your business? What is in it for you?

- What does success look like for you with this business?

CHAPTER 4

Self-Discipline

With self-discipline most anything is possible.
–Theodore Roosevelt

In this chapter:
  • Identify tools to build self-discipline.
  • Uncover the driving forces of procrastination and how to beat them.
  • Increase productivity.

It's cold and dark outside and your bed is cozy and warm. You didn't sleep well, and it feels like you only closed your eyes moments ago, but the alarm is blaring and poof, it's morning.

You think about all the reasons why maybe you'll just skip today but there they are: your workout clothes. You laid them out last night before lying down and you curse yourself for knowing you would think about skipping this training.

As you get up, the dog comes running in, tail wagging, knowing that it's time to go. As you stumble outside and take in that first deep breath of the crisp air, you smile and give yourself a little mental high-five and get busy with your training. Because you know the time you put in today will pay off in the future.

Entrepreneurs need the same discipline as the endurance athlete — with or without the wagging-tailed dog.

Self-discipline: *the ability to make yourself do things that should be done. (Merriam-Webster)*

Self-discipline is an intentional use of time, energy, and resources to create the outcomes that are important to you. When you apply this principle and skill in your life, you will see great forward movement in the results you produce — in your business, or in any facet of your life.

This essential quality of an entrepreneur fuels our ability to do the work, especially on the things and at the times you don't have a great desire to do them. That is true self-discipline.

Entrepreneurship is a human-driven engine. Much like a mechanical engine that powers a vehicle, the primary function of the human engine is to move a vehicle (the business) forward in the most efficient and effective way.

In their business, an entrepreneur is both the human engine of their vehicle, plus the mechanic and the driver. As the mechanic, you keep your vehicle at peak performance. As the driver, you steer (set the direction) while accelerating the vehicle along its paths. The human engine has more nuances and complexities than a mechanical one ever encounters, which creates the need for specific tools.

The most important and powerful of these is self-discipline.

The effort needed to grow an idea and share it with the world takes tremendous self-discipline. At the beginning of the journey, when there is no audience, when you're working toward a future only you can see, your excitement for the idea is your catalyst, and your self-discipline to see it through is your main fuel source.

Many great ideas never see the market because the entrepreneur lacked the necessary discipline — the continual ability to do the things that need to be done even when you don't want to do them. It is an essential skill for being both boss and worker in one person.

Self-discipline is not just about getting the hard or boring things done; it is also about pushing yourself to go further than you think you can go. It is about the ability to both self-motivate and self-actualize to bring your idea to market.

The full force of this state at its peak drives you to move beyond your perceived limits and break through to the levels of success you desire. The discipline to do the uncomfortable thing is sometimes the only tool you will have to enable you to reach that next level.

Another aspect of self-discipline — focus — comes into play here. The successful entrepreneur, who sees opportunity everywhere they look, must exhibit great discipline to avoid being distracted by shiny object syndrome (SOS) and stay focused on the tasks, projects, and ideas that are most important.

To pursue the one goal — to do that one thing only, and as well as you possibly can — takes dedication and single-mindedness. The best entrepreneurs will have more opportunities than they can ever possibly accomplish in one lifetime. The successful ones learn to discern what is theirs to pursue and let the other shiny possibilities float by for another to accomplish. This takes major discipline.

How Do You Build Self-Discipline?

If you are not naturally self-disciplined, all is not lost. Most of us don't begin with this skill fully formed — we must learn and strengthen it. Much like a muscle that needs focused exercise and stretching to become strong.

We only need to look to the military to see that self-discipline is a characteristic any of us can develop. The military is famous for their process that makes entire elite teams through building discipline by routines, structure, and physical and mental challenges. It is often a space where many people who lacked self-discipline or focus have grown and increased tremendously.

There are two distinct parts to self-discipline: perception and dedication.

There are some that argue the best way to build discipline is to challenge what you think you are capable of — your perception — through physical tests. Many successful entrepreneurs continually stretch the perception of their limits through endurance or extreme competitions. Crossing a finish line you once felt was impossible, lifting an amount of weight that exceeds your previous expectations, or even accomplishing more work in a short time — all leave imprints in the brain.

Using a tangible goal to work towards also helps build self-discipline over time, through dedication. Pursuing a goal that requires dedication creates discipline. It is said that champions (in athletic circles) are made when no one is looking; this is also true for entre-preneurs.

Having a competition or deadline to test one's limits is equally im-portant for this method because people need to feel their progress, or they will quit. It is a powerful reminder that hard work pays off. Those opportunities are rare in entrepreneurial ventures, so build-ing them elsewhere in your life is helpful.

For most people to develop self-discipline, it's unnecessary for them to push themselves to a breaking point like in the military or endurance competitions. Focusing on development is key. You can create self-discipline through the simple (but not always easy!) act of small consistent efforts to show up and doing the thing you need to do to reach your goal. It is sometimes doing the task you hate be-cause it just needs to be done. As the entrepreneur — tag, you're it! — you're likely the best one, or perhaps the only one to do it!

Most importantly, *self-discipline is about keeping your word to your-self.* It's about accomplishing the things you deem most important to you, your business, and those in your life. It is unfortunate that studies show that as humans we are better at keeping our word to others than we are to ourselves. But we can fix that.

The key to enhancing self-discipline is your commitment to devel-oping this skill. As an entrepreneur, this commitment falls to you. There is no drill sergeant or boss to motivate or require this. Suc-cessful entrepreneurs must provide this for themselves. If this is not something you grew up with or comes easily to you, you must put in the work and practice regularly.

The following sections offer some tools to help you do just that.

Take Choice Out

One of the best ways to build self-discipline is to set up routines and schedules. Yes, this then requires the self-discipline to stick to the schedule you set — but stay with me.

Having a schedule takes choice out of the equation. Your decision in the moment is the weakest part of discipline. For example, at this very moment, I sit at a desk at 6:30am because at this time each morning I have dedicated (and scheduled) 90 minutes to writing this book. Writing is not easy for me, so I have a tendency to procrastinate. By setting a writing schedule, I remove choice as long as I follow the plan.

When I simply put writing on my to-do list and didn't schedule time, I found many excuses not to do it, instead working on other things. But once I had it on my schedule, the writing miraculously got completed. I just followed my schedule, wrote when I scheduled myself to do so, and stopped when it was time for my next activity or task. And this book is the result.

Self-discipline ensures you make time to complete the things that need to be done. Routines and schedules allow you to anticipate what is next and prepare to be in the best mindset to accomplish it. It also allows you to understand a timeframe and that alone can sometimes make a dreaded task easier. Anyone can do something for X amount of time, right?!

As you set your schedule to include those things that must be done, it is important to recognize your personal rhythm: when you are most creative, most innovative, most productive — and also laziest. Preparing your schedule to harmonize as best as you can with your natural tendencies will help you succeed here.

When you set a routine for yourself, you may also find that your mind quickly adapts to the program. You may find that it becomes easier to get the task done because you are in the right mindset to accomplish it.

Scheduling known or recurring tasks is a great way to create an environment for self-discipline.

Someone once asked Somerset Maugham if he wrote on a schedule or only when struck by inspiration. "I write only when inspiration strikes," he replied. "Fortunately, it strikes every morning at nine o'clock sharp." [1]

Defeat Procrastination

In his book *The War of Art*, Steven Pressfield states, "Procrastination is the most common manifestation of resistance because it's the easiest to rationalize. We don't tell ourselves, 'I'm never going to write that book.' Instead we say, 'I'm going to do it tomorrow.' And tomorrow never comes."

Self-discipline is the key to addressing procrastination when moving towards your goals as an entrepreneur.

Procrastination takes many forms, and each is equally deadly to your success. Whether it shows up as avoidance because of overwhelm or not knowing how to tackle something or distraction through need or escape — procrastination in any form delays or limits success.

Procrastination will test even the most self-disciplined. You must notice the way procrastination shows up for you and build methods to address it when you experience the desire.

There is a story that a famous author used to joke that the way to start writing a new book is to first start your laundry, then do the dishes... When writing this book, I certainly felt the urge to do some serious housework, and I don't even have a house!

No one is immune to procrastination. The trick is this: do you notice what you do when you procrastinate? Because then you can stop that activity and get back on track with your important work. I notice that when I'm procrastinating or feeling overwhelmed, I start looking at email. Sorting and responding to email gives me little wins each time I press the delete button, but it does not help the project I'm trying to move forward. Since I learned to recognize this tendency in myself, I've been able to catch myself when it occurs, and return to the work at hand.

Eliminating or Reducing Distraction

As stated earlier, self-discipline is about intentionally focused attention toward a result. Therefore, anything that is not an intentional use of time is likely a distraction. The most successful entrepreneurs are very protective of their time, and mindless uses of time are not part of their success habits.

Time is the most precious human asset. Time is the one commodity that cannot be bought, manufactured, or manipulated. Being self-disciplined about the use of their time is how successful entrepreneurs accomplish great things. To not use one's time judiciously has costs, for all of us.

It is unlikely you will ever see Warren Buffett or Bill Gates spending a lot of time scrolling through Instagram, checking how many followers they have or the number of likes on a particular post. These activities do not move their goals forward; they are non-essential distractions.

The challenge for entrepreneurs is that some of the very things that can be distractions are necessary in the early stages of a venture. It is the discipline to do the necessary work and not get sucked into the distraction portion that is the key.

At some point, you will be able to pass along to others the items that could be distractions for you and remove the risk altogether. Until then, you must practice self-discipline to protect your most precious asset: your time.

Darren Hardy identifies that a distraction causes a loss of 23.5 minutes of productivity. Just the buzz of a notification is all it takes to break flow or train of thought. The flash of an email or the stop at the doorway of your office — even if you say you don't have five minutes to talk now — will cost you valuable time to get back into full concentration. Multiply this by each distraction all day and you've lost tremendous amounts of productivity!

In the beginning stages of entrepreneurship, often only one or two people work in your business. The internal distractions are more likely necessary to keep all the plates spinning at the same time and making sure they don't hit the floor and break.

As business grows, distractions will come from both internal and external sources. You'll have clients to maintain and address and staff to direct, correct, and monitor.

Meetings are the number one accepted distraction in the world of business. Research by Harvard Business School and Boston University shows that 71% of meetings are unnecessary and unproductive.[2] And many meetings — even necessary ones — are longer than needed to obtain the objective.

The great entrepreneurs of today hold hard and fast rules about attending meetings and for meetings to be called in their companies.

Steve Jobs was famous for making sure the only people at a meeting were critical to the outcome and asked individuals to leave for this reason. Sheryl Sandberg reportedly crosses off agenda items throughout a meeting, and as soon as the team completes all items, she calls the meeting to an end even if it was scheduled for longer.

These are just a few examples of how successful businesspeople protect their time. It is important to understand that sometimes the distraction comes from within the company and is disguised as work. Be aware and create systems to prevent distractions in your business. Doing so will create more time for your business and its real priorities.

Keystone Habits

In his book *The Power of Habit*, Charles Duhigg discusses and defines the term keystone habit. This is a habit that creates a natural inclination to other positive actions or results. Like the other skills of emotional intelligence you'll develop with this book, self-discipline is an excellent example of a keystone habit.

The habits you practice in your business will also show up elsewhere in your life. As you become more self-disciplined in your business, you will find that you become more self-disciplined in your personal life. Any of the systems you've put into place to organize and run your business days will tend to show up in the way you manage your personal responsibilities.

Self-discipline as a keystone habit will affect everything important in your life — from maintaining relationships with friends, to healthy eating or exercise, and so much more. As you stay committed in one area of your life, it becomes a pattern to commit in other areas.

Of all the skills in this book, self-awareness and self-discipline are the most foundational to your success in business and in life, and to the other skills in this book as well.

Putting Self-Discipline to Work

Self-discipline and having singlemindedness towards the success of your business is imperative. As an entrepreneur, you must ensure your focus on your business is directed intentionally and benefits the goals you have.

As a human being, recognize that "no person is an island," and that there are other equally or more important things in your life, which will sometimes create conflict between the needs of your business and the needs of your personal life.

Take the time to look carefully at the complete picture of your life during this process and don't assume that your personal life will hold forever as you incessantly nurture your business. If you are in a relationship, have children, family, and friends, or take part in a community of any kind, you must not forget their importance in your life.

Sometimes the discipline you need is to take a break from working to attend to the other parts of your life.

Do not allow the time, dedication, and discipline required to making your business a success cause you to neglect your personal life. We will talk about the dangers of this further along in the book, but for now, know that no business, idea, money, status, or success will replace the people who are important to you.

Self-discipline is about utilizing your resources in the most productive way. It is about intentionality and purpose as a human force in your business.

Having this skill will provide the fuel to move an initiative forward, to weather the storms and to accomplish the necessary and less desirable tasks in pursuit of the end goal.

There are systems, resources, and tools that can help you create and maintain your discipline, but you must learn to determine where you need them and the dedication of regularly employing them. Self-discipline is a muscle you can train and strengthen over time to produce the maximum results from the resources you have available. Once you master this, you will find your efforts rewarded with greater productivity and consistent, measurable progress.

Self-Discipline Exercises

How Is Your Self-Discipline?

Rate yourself on a scale of 1–5 (one being Rarely, five being Always):

- I easily keep commitments to myself, on their original timeline.
- I have no trouble keeping motivated on long-range goals.
- I enjoy having a set routine and daily schedule.

Procrastination and Distraction

- What is your preferred method of distraction or procrastination? (You may have several, depending on the task or situation you're trying to avoid.)
- Do you have a pattern of situations that trigger procrastination? (example: overwhelm)
- Are there any situations where you don't experience procrastination? Are there common factors in those situations?

Methods to Build Self-Discipline

- Set a timer for a short amount of time so you only have enough to start a task, and either continue when the timer sounds or stop and repeat at a later time.
- Set small goals for accomplishing only one piece of the item to be completed.
- Create accountability with a partner or group.

CHAPTER 5

Understanding and Managing Risk

In this chapter:
- Evaluate your risk tolerance.
- Understand the art of risk.
- Identify tools for managing risk.

Walking into the popular Blockbuster headquarters in 2000, Reed Hastings of the startup Netflix arrived to discuss a partnership opportunity between the two companies. Some of you may not even know who Blockbuster is, but I'm sure you know Netflix.

Once a giant and the leader in the video rental market, Blockbuster heard from Hastings a radical new opportunity for evolving its business. This new idea — DVD by mail — was costly for Blockbuster, since it was a different model from their retail stores. And it would drastically cut into one of the company's biggest revenue generator at the time: the customer-dreaded, late-return fee.

Because of internal conflicts with investors around revenue and operational model changes, Blockbuster declined the Netflix partnership. In the next few years, Blockbuster did not move fast enough or meet the customer's needs in the way competitors like Netflix did, and it cost them. Blockbuster filed for bankruptcy in 2010, and eventually all (but one) 9,000 Blockbuster stores went out of business. Today, Netflix has taken Blockbuster's place as the royalty of streaming entertainment because they took a risk on a new model — and Blockbuster didn't.

Risk and Gambling

The definition of risk: 1. chance of something going wrong; 2. possibility of investment loss; 3. Statistical odds of danger.

Entrepreneurship is synonymous with risk. But risk is not the same as gambling, where "the house" wins most of the time. Entrepreneurship bestows success to those who understand how to play the game to their ultimate benefit. This means understanding the game and being able to withstand loss.

There is no part in your entrepreneurial journey that will not include some risk. How you manage that risk determines the level of success you will have as an entrepreneur.

Risk will show up in all aspects of your business and understanding your risk personality, and that of those affected by your risks, will benefit your stress level and mental health. As we discuss throughout the book, self-assessment will be critical to managing this effectively.

Taking risks is an art form and when it works out in your favor, it is as beautiful as a well-choreographed ballet. When it doesn't, it feels like an awkward teenaged boy at his first school dance.

There are many emotion-based elements that play a part in the outcome of a risk. Tolerance, analysis, personality, and fear all intersect in this one heightened occurrence.

Risk Tolerance and Your Comfort Zone

The first thing to understand about risk is your tolerance. Risk tolerance is the degree of uncertainty you are willing to take on to achieve potentially greater rewards. Each person is different and in each area of life may have varying levels of acceptable risk. All risk is not equal, and it is important to know where you stand in each area before the situation arises. Risk will always push the boundaries of your comfort zone.

Understanding your tolerance is not an excuse to avoid stepping outside your comfort zone. It is to identify where you may need support and what resources you may need. Because the risk you take on in some circumstances may affect others, from investors and co-workers to family members and significant others, understanding the risk tolerance of all parties is important.

Depending on the risk and the potential negative outcome (the downside), asking yourself clarifying questions will help you decide where you stand in any situation.

In his book *Creative Calling,* Chase Jarvis explains, "Each of us has to find the middle ground between faith and doubt and learn to get comfortable there." Getting comfortable in that uncertain middle ground is a key challenge in creating what the world does not yet see.

You will be unable to avoid risk at any stage of your business. Understanding your tolerance in each situation and managing the risk based on your tolerance will put you in a better position to handle the many challenges you will face.

It's the big ideas that change lives and create lasting impact — but more than one entrepreneur has gone down in flames because although their idea might have been great and timely, in their exuberance they overlooked or didn't prepare for the "what if it doesn't work" part of the equation.

You will take bold risks as an entrepreneur — but knowing how to assess risk is the difference between business and gambling.
–Elizabeth Miner

Risk Is an Art

Risk is not a science, as some believe. It is a living and breathing, fluid form of art. In entrepreneurship the landscape is dynamic, and the effects of risk vary.

Risk by its very nature is unpredictable. Managing risk relies on the hypothesis of how any decision may play out. Understand that hypothesis is a fancy word for an educated guess!

Risk has two sides: opportunity and failure, and countless variations within each. To accept a risk is to accept any degree of success or failure that results from a decision. It is rarely a total win or total loss.

Risks taken are often what shape a business and highlight its unique qualities. When an entrepreneur builds a business disrupting an industry or iterating in a current market, that is a brand-defining risk. Playing in this arena brings incredible opportunity; it can also bring the possibility of extraordinary loss.

The very reason to build a business is to do something different in the marketplace. Being an entrepreneur is being an artist and creating something new. Risk is the admission charge to play the game and precedes any reward in this arena.

Protect the Downside

The goal, as many successful entrepreneurs will explain, is to mitigate risk. You will not win every time. Those who regularly take risks recognize that is not possible. The underlying principle is to not lose as much as you win. This principle identifies there will be losses.

One of the most famous risk-takers of the current time is Richard Branson. He wrote in his autobiography, *Losing My Virginity*, "It is only by being bold that you get anywhere. If you are a risk-taker, then the art is to protect the downside."

To mitigate risk, or protect the downside, it is important to understand the full magnitude of what is at stake and calculate the effect of a loss.

Warren Buffett has admittedly lost millions of dollars in investments over the years; he has borne the consequences of any risk he takes because of the balance process he uses to hedge risk consequences. Knowing what is at risk and planning a counter strategy is an approach that obviously has worked well for him!

With a complete picture of the best-possible and worst-possible scenarios, one can make an effective decision, based on their risk tolerance and how much they can protect against, mitigate, or tolerate the downside.

Confirmation Bias

The problem so many have with managing risk is they tend to focus heavily on one side of the risk/reward equation.

When a person is so worried about the potential negative consequence of a particular risk, they often cannot assess optimistically because of their fear. The alternative of concentrating only on the positive outcome of a risk is equally limiting to an assessment because of the potential blind spots this can create.

Ultimately, the result of taking any risk is rarely the full upside or downside; the results will often be degrees of either.

Regardless, when you focus either on the gloom or the glory, your assessment will be lopsided. It is in these circumstances that asking for help can fill in some blind spots and round out your assessment. Ray Dalio suggests in his book *Principles* that if you are looking for the best answer only through your own eyes, you will be "terribly handicapped."

Risk History

Each of us has a personal relationship with risk. From the time we were little and learning about our environment through basic discovery, to every time we attempted a new skill, we encountered risk.

The benefit of being children is that we learned and attempted (most often) under the watchful eyes of people who cared about our success. Those same watchful eyes might have removed many obstacles to make our path as smooth as possible.

It is usually those same caring people who helped us develop our initial understanding of risk and whether it was something to fear or embrace. This imprint from our early memories is often what we carry through the years.

Although we have been given a powerful impression of risk, it does not mean that we cannot work with it. If, as you begin your entrepreneurial journey, your risk tolerance is low, you will either opt out of this path altogether, or you will need to expand it.

When you understand your feelings about risk — and keep in mind they can vary considerably based on what is at risk — then you can begin to understand your risk profile.

The meaning you give a result may depend on what is at stake. This will affect your behavior around any particular risk. Knowing the meaning you give a result may help you understand how it can influence decision-making.

Remember, there is no good or bad history; there is only understanding yourself. By doing so, you will better position yourself to seek advice and take the steps necessary for a well-rounded evaluation.

Taking risks with the knowledge of the stories that create your relationship with risk will allow you to better prepare for any outcome.

When It All Goes Terribly Wrong

How you handle when things don't turn out the way you wanted is an emotional matter. This needs to be addressed because you will have failures throughout your journey.

You may or may not be comfortable with loss, but you must be willing to sit with it long enough to learn its lesson. The knowledge gained from a studying why things didn't turn out the way you want is the silver lining in a loss or failure.

The exact reason to understand your relationship with risk is to be in the best position at these times when things don't end up the way you expected or wanted. Knowing what you need to maintain steady leadership in the face of failure will minimize further damage.

To strip failure of its real emotional consequence is to scrub the concepts of grit and resilience of the very qualities that make them both so important: toughness, doggedness and perseverance.
–Brené Brown

There is often so much more to be learned from failure than success. And we only realize the benefits of a failure when we take time to sift through the ashes. The ability to clearly assess the process, the prediction, and outcome is where the gold lies.

This is the time to analyze what the anticipated risks and the actual risks were and to determine if, how, and why they vary. To delve into the predicted outcome versus the reality will provide useful information on any short-sightedness or accuracy and likely provide a direction for future situations.

Ray Dalio uses an issue log at the company he founded, Bridgewater Associates. The purpose of the log is to identify patterns and metrics that are helpful as learning tools, to avoid repeating the same mistake in the future.

The act of surviving a failure has its own important benefits. Understand that even after the most epic disasters, when it appears as though all has been lost, there are still rewards. Knowledge is one. So is the resilience that comes from surviving a failure or adversity. Both can serve as springboards for your next opportunity.

Evaluating the data for successful or failed risks is one way to continue to learn about your behaviors, biases, and processes. When you assess all elements, you can create strategy and systems for future circumstances. The Risk Evaluation at the end of this chapter is just one example of how you might approach this.

You and Risk

Everything comes back to self-awareness because risk triggers emotions. It is critical to understand the history you bring into the business and what stories from your past may play into the way you manage risk.

The most pivotal moments in a business can bring up the most painful memories and stories. Dealing with proving value, worthiness, etc. can have a major role in effective risk management.

Rewriting these stories to remove their power over you is a process well worth the effort. Separating business from personal history will allow clarity to evaluate a risk for exactly what it is. This process strips the meaning from the outcome, allowing you to make a pure assessment.

Sometimes memories and the stories they create will not be evident ahead of time; for those situations, as you come upon them, it is essential that you make the time to move through them. For others, just reading this segment may have prompted your awareness.

When you come across a situation that you actually feel in your body, you know there is something there to explore. These signals may be obvious or subtle, but do not ignore them.

Addressing a painful memory that has caused you to act in certain ways when it in the face of risk is not easy. This is a time where I recommend enlisting the help of a professional.

Take the time to complete this step and you will disempower the past, one story at a time. This process will allow you a straightforward assessment and the best decision you can make for your business without dragging your past along.

Time After Time

Risk-taking is something that gets easier over time. Although the stakes may be higher as time goes on, if you do this work, your ability to refine your process will likely improve.

Risk-taking is an entrepreneurial muscle that will strengthen over time and with use. It is important to practice assessment processes often to keep the skill sharp even when there are not immediate opportunities before you.

When you practice evaluating risks, you don't have to use your own. We live in an age of information and there are sources everywhere that will provide you information regarding a risk that you can use for practice.

Every annual report a public company produces for its stockholders always contains a section on risk. Evaluating the risks identified in a similar company or industry is a brilliant method to practice and see how things play out over time for another without ever having to face the risk yourself. Doing this practice also provides you insights into future risks for your own business — you will have already walked them through your process and will be better prepared.

Being able to trust your process and be comfortable with it is a priceless benefit.

Managing Others' Risk Tolerance

We've established that knowing your risk tolerance and your relationship to it is critical to working in a way that you feel most confident. This takes great self-awareness and personal work to allow you to be in the best state to move forward in an environment where so much is unknown.

The next step is to understand how the risks you take affect others around you, from those in your business to those in your personal life. The stress that other people may feel from choices they have little or no control over but might affect their lives is real. You should not ignore this issue.

Assuming that those around you will understand why you took the risk when it all works out positively ignores the discomfort they may feel and its effects on their lives. Assuming a risk will work out positively also negates others' opportunity to prepare themselves for what might happen.

Keeping a risk secret from others is not the answer to not affecting them — it causes more harm than good all around. It is important to cultivate the ability to share the knowledge you have (to the extent you can) with those who might be affected by your decision.

Betting the house (literally) when someone else relies on living in that house means that your risk is not solely your own. This means that a risk that actually puts a critical element of someone's needs in jeopardy deserves consideration.

I'm not saying don't take risks because others are uncomfortable. The very part of being an entrepreneur is seeing something others do not yet see, so it is very possible that others won't understand some risks you feel called to take.

What I mean is that you have an obligation to help others understand why you may put something they value in a position to be lost. Share how you are managing the possibility of negative consequences to help them understand the full picture so they too might feel more comfortable with the steps you've taken.

Risk is inherent in your journey as an entrepreneur. You have accepted and chosen to move through it. Remember that stress created in your life affects others and take care to acknowledge and address it as much as possible.

Tools for Managing Risk

Mentors

Risk management is not a skill taught in school and is not something most people are taught anywhere. People often develop their methods through experience or, as I mentioned earlier, have others' experiences impressed upon them.

One of the many areas where mentors are invaluable is helping you develop the skills of risk management. Find a mentor who is adept at managing risk downside and able to walk away from exciting-but-out-of-scope risks and you will increase your success in this area exponentially.

Mentors have the benefit of experience that can increase your knowledge on which you base your assessment. They will also provide a trusted additional viewpoint to provide a broader picture of an opportunity.

Mentors can be incredibly helpful in other areas besides risk management, but few other helpers have the mentor's depth of experience in this area. As we will talk about in greater detail in chapter 12, mentors who have developed their tools and found their way to manage risk can be one of your greatest resources.

Legal Options

Legal tools are sometimes a useful method to protect the downside of risk. A legal document won't remove all negative consequences, but it's a valuable tool for detailing the outcome of "what ifs."

There are many products a legal professional can provide to help navigate some risks at each stage of business. Legal documents are also prime methods to detail your intentions for how you'll handle future successes.

The time to implement legal tools is before entering into any risk. Use this tool to define what is at stake and how each person is expected to behave, benefit from, and share in a gain or loss. This is the space to use professionals because a well-written document can avoid major issues or assumptions.

From Non-Disclosure Agreements (NDAs) to Initial Public Offerings (IPOs) these documents can act like a roadmap for those involved. Even having the conversations necessary to put the documents together is an important step in understanding all sides of an opportunity.

A legal professional is also tremendously helpful with risk evaluation. This is an area of business that is costly however, what it can avoid or deter is far more expensive in most cases.

I cannot stress enough that you connect with counsel as early as possible in your journey so you know the person you can call on in need. Leaving this choice to a time when you have a situation to address may not allow you the ability to find a good fit for your needs.

Precedent

No one today is inventing the wheel.

In every industry there will be those who have come before you and built a similar business or worked on solving a similar problem. Both success and failure will always provide information that is helpful.

Today information is plentiful and it's important to make use of other's experiences. Articles, books, interviews, and biographical data are all available and hold a wealth of information that can act as a form of mentorship.

Learning about how others have approached a similar business risk and managed their companies during both good and bad times is useful education. Because stories are often made public after an event, you review the full picture of what happened. Make use of this information and others' examples.

An entrepreneur can learn so much from studying how other people have made decisions, handled risk, created a new market, or managed a crowded or established one. Many successful entrepreneurs want to help others blaze their own trail and we gain so much by researching their journey.

Looking to businesses that have failed has tremendous learning potential. Ignoring lessons from previous misjudgments or errors is a waste of a good failure. No matter if the studied business is in a similar market or not, some information is universal to business and can be beneficial to you.

When beginning a new business, one must start by understanding the landscape that exists before they build. Research as much as possible about the companies in the field and read their 10ks and annual reports, if published, to see the risks they anticipate.

If others are in the marketplace you desire to enter, know that this is likely a positive sign there is a market. There will always be a market for more than one company in a field and the one that makes a great product or service will always have customers.

If others are not in the marketplace you desire or are no longer there, research those companies to find out why. The best failure is the one you can learn from without having to experience it personally. There will be clues to what might have caused the business to fail that you can use to either rethink yours or avoid by knowing.

Precedent is valuable and available in many formats. Make use of this tool to help you manage risks others have taken. Use the history available to create the best future for your business as possible.

Building Your Risk Tolerance

Entrepreneurship involves risk. To put yourself in the best position to make smart, calculated choices, you must build your awareness of all aspects of who and how the risks affect all involved. Thinking through these elements before acting will put you in the best place to make successful choices.

Managing risk is not simply about protecting your downside; it is knowing and understanding the way you approach risk and planning, assessing and protecting in the best interest of your company and client. It is about doing well in business while bringing changes to market.

Being prepared to address such a mainstay of business as risk in your journey has an incredible advantage not taught in any entrepreneurial program. Working through your thoughts and relationship to risk is your EQ advantage.

To improve your skill of taking risks, you must have experience and the emotional resilience to move through the practice. This is a muscle that gets stronger as you exercise it — keep this in mind as you move through this journey.

Risk Tolerance Exercises

Risk Relationship Profile

- What are your early experiences with risk? Were you the daredevil kid or did you fear getting hurt or taking uncalculated chances?

- What are your biggest fears or discomforts about taking risks?

- What is one story you remember about taking a risk? How did it turn out for you and how did it make you feel?

Risk Assessment Questions

- What is at risk to lose? What is the possible gain?

- Is a loss recoverable?

- What are the variations of outcomes possible?

- How much time or money will it take to make up for a bad outcome?

- What will it look like if I walk away from this risk/opportunity?

Risk Evaluation

- Create a chart with the following categories:

Perceived Risk	Actual Risk
Analysis Done	Analysis Missed
Information Sources	Information Overlooked
Controlled Circumstances	Unknown Variables

- Once you've completed the chart, review and answer these questions:

- What do you wish you would have known?

- How could you have known this information?

- What was the best thing you did during the initial analysis for this risk?

CHAPTER 6

Decision-Making

In this chapter:
- Choose your analysis method.
- Identify decision dangers.
- Defeat decision fatigue.

As an entrepreneur, you will face innumerable decisions. Your ability to be a strong decision maker is paramount to your success.

This skill is not as black and white as it sounds. It is not as simple as yes or no. Decision-making entails the ability to synthesize information, to know how a decision will affect your business, customers, and staff, to anticipate the drain or gain on your business and to manage risk.

This, like risk, is an art form more than a skill and an entrepreneur is best served by being able to work in many different media. As we know, art can be taught, but to become an artist, one has to practice.

An important note to remember is that no one gets every decision correct and to know this going into the process is both helpful and daunting.

To take a line from the legal world, "time is of the essence" when making decisions. Take too long to analyze your situation and the information presented and you may lose the opportunity. Take too little time to gather enough data to assess the risk and you may make a decision that is not in the best interest of the company, staff, or customer.

Everyone has an opinion about what you should do and there will be times when you will listen to many or all of them. It is important to learn how to decipher if and to whom you need to reach out for input in a particular situation. A mentor may be of significant support here, but keep in mind that the decision rests with you in the end.

The number of decisions to be made when running a company is tremendous and for some can become problematic. There is a real thing called decision fatigue and the environment of entrepreneurship is ripe for this dilemma. Managing the onslaught of decisions required is key to reducing the burden on the entrepreneur.

To say that you will be the person at the top and bottom of the hill for every decision is an understatement. The stress that comes with a regular barrage of choices is plentiful and attitude is everything. Managing the fear, stress, and ego responses during decision-making is a proficiency that is rarely discussed or taught in business classes.

Knowing you will fail and make a poor decision from time to time is important — knowing how to handle it when you do is even more important. Taking the responsibility for a poor decision is the true mark of a leader. Taking responsibility is not enough; a great leader controls the damage a poor decision causes by acting swiftly to limit the negative effects and correct what is possible.

Sometimes the results of a decision will fall into a gray area. The results may not be great, but they may not be terrible either — and those are almost more difficult to deal with than a clear hit or miss.

Some outcomes will simply require redirection or modification; others will need to be thrown out altogether.

Decision-making at the helm of a company is both the benefit and burden of an entrepreneur. On one hand, you have an unparalleled capability to determine the direction of the company — which is what you dreamed about. On the other hand, you — and sometimes you alone — have the responsibility of the decisions that shape the company and its future. This can be tremendously stressful.

In this chapter, we will explore how successful entrepreneurs have navigated the labyrinth of this aspect of entrepreneurship and provide ideas for you to put into place to triumph in this important area.

Analyzing Before Deciding

All decisions require some degree of analysis, and people handle this in all different ways. Many are fans of a pros-and-cons list to see if a decision will have more benefit than detriment. Some people are "gut" deciders who feel an intuitive guidance and go with their feeling about matters. Some make decisions quickly and some do methodical research before drawing a conclusion.

There is no right or wrong method for making good decisions. No one method will be perfect for all situations. You must develop the ability to call on the appropriate method for the various circumstances you will face.

The Pros-and-Cons Approach

Making a list of the benefits and disadvantages of a particular decision is a method many people use for making big decisions. Most times, this method is little more than a guessing game based on the list creator's assumptions.

The key problem with this method of assessment is that it is difficult for humans not to be biased for one choice. In those situations, the pro or con list may be easier for the list maker to imagine.

The way our human minds carry bias will cause the desired confirmation, whether we want it or not. Information bias will color our ability to think of the results not wanted and make it difficult to make an accurate list for or against a particular decision without input from others.

Even in best-case scenarios this, like all methods, is simply an educated guess. On each side of the list will be hypotheses, which in most cases we cannot prove true or false until we make the decision.

The primary benefit of this method is that we clearly document our thought process. If we gather and study the data following the outcome of a decision made in this manner, we can learn a lot from either positive or negative outcomes.

If you are a person who is visual and benefits from seeing an opportunity laid out before you, this might be a method you find most helpful. Remember that this method can be time consuming and biased without additional input.

Sometimes, it's difficult to know when we've exhausted all the potential outcomes and the time has come to make a decision. If you are using this type of decision-making, be aware of your personal tendencies, as this process can lead to procrastination. Set limits on how long you will spend in this process and you will avoid the never-ending list.

Remember, you will never have all the information you need to make the perfect decision. Your goal is to make the best decision possible with the information available to you in a given time frame.

Some Pros-and-Cons List Suggestions

Before the Decision:

- Set a timeline for research.

- Review data with opposing view holders.

After the Decision:

- Review collected data.

- Analyze any glaring holes in data or process.

- Record key points of success or failure for future reference.

The "From the Gut" Approach

Making decisions "from the gut" is how many people begin their business. For some, this is a great success for them personally, but this method impossible to scale, as these decisions have no set process by which another can follow.

This style has many other issues besides scale. When managing by intuition, you must receive clear signals regularly, not clouded by stress, fear, desires, or any other human traits that might color your view.

Intuition has a place in decision-making, and in combination with other methods, can lead you to take bold chances others may have avoided. Intuition can help direct you to challenge information you're receiving. It can help you be more cautious or bolder for no obvious reason. But unless your intuition is thoroughly attuned, it can and will be swayed by emotion.

When a situation works out differently than you expect, it can affect your confidence in your instinct for future decisions. Once you lose faith in your ability to trust your gut, how do you make decisions then?

A strong self-awareness may help prevent misunderstandings of your gut feelings, and help you understand when to use it, and when not to. Your intuition is a difficult element to trust on every occasion, so while adding it to your toolbox of decision-making skills is good, relying on intuition as the sole source of guidance is not.

Finally, intuition tends to concentrate decision-making with just one gut – the owner's. Managing a company where only one person can make decisions creates a bottleneck and can lead to stagnation. As the company grows, this issue will increase, leading to disruption of process and progress when the decision maker is not available.

Having only one person capable of doing any major task is dangerous to the longevity of a business. Placing on the entrepreneur the sole ability and responsibility to make all the decisions in a company is far beyond "key man." Avoid this.

The Consensus Approach

As ineffective as it is to have only one person making decisions for your business, so too is including everyone. It may seem like the democratic resolution to the stress of making all the decisions yourself, but it has its own challenges.

Seeking the input and insight of others is important while making decisions, but listening to everyone is a problem. Limit input those who will be credible and helpful for moving the process forward. If you involve too many people in company decisions, a reverse bottleneck may occur: no one reaches agreement and so no decisions are made, or are made very slowly.

Instead, seek a happy-medium when looking to share decision-making in your business. You might opt for a board of directors/

advisory committee approach, where select small groups make decisions in their area of expertise.

Regardless of what you decide, making sure you clearly define a process is critical to managing both expectations and results. Make sure everyone involved knows when they have a role in a decision — and when they do not so they do not interfere.

Some Consensus Suggestions:

- Define your process for consensus decision-making.
- Assign areas of responsibility to members or committees.
- Set time limits for discussion.
- Define decision boundaries and metrics.

Time Is of the Essence

In the world of entrepreneurship, everything seems to move really fast and really slow all at the same time. Time is one of the most precious resources for the entrepreneur (perhaps the most precious), and when making decisions, time can feel like the countdown clock on a game show.

Take too long making analysis and getting feedback on a potential decision and the opportunity can disappear or can change altogether. Having all the information possible to make the best decision will never come; this reality can cause difficulty for some entrepreneurs.

The challenge is to gather enough information and input to make an educated decision and move on it. Remember, too: you don't have to do all the information gathering or analysis alone. If you are short on time and need to sift through a significant amount of information or resources, identify people on your team or whom you trust with the right skill sets to review and summarize a piece of the information to consider.

When time is a factor, address the challenge by assessing what you need to make an informed decision and filling those needs.

Some Analysis Parameter Suggestions

- Define your decision timeline.

- Determine the most critical aspects of a decision to focus on.

- Divide data collection or analysis if necessary.

- Determine if you have enough data to make an educated decision.

The key question you'll wrestle with in any of these methods is: how much is enough information? There is no easy answer, and each situation will be different. The balance to strike is this: efficiently assess as much data as possible to reach the best-informed decision, while avoiding a key pitfall: perfection.

Beware Perfectionism

Attempting to make the perfect decision with all the information needed will elude you and lead to missed opportunities. Figure out how to manage your perfectionism early in your entrepreneurial journey. The tools you learned in chapter 3 will be helpful here.

I'm not advocating mediocre as the answer; your aim is always for excellence. Excellence is achievable; perfection is not.

At the core of most people's desire for perfection is fear.

Some of these fears are baseless; some derive from specific emotional stories from our experiences. Regardless of its origin, the desire to be perfect can derail you as an entrepreneur. Dealing with the cause of your perfectionism and releasing its hold on you will benefit your business and other areas of your life.

You may best handle this process with the support of a professional therapist or counselor — consider it a sound investment in your business. If you don't address it, perfectionism will continue to show up in your business and will hold you back from the very excellence you seek.

Procrastination is a reliable sign that perfection is at play. Many delay doing something they feel they are not good at to avoid the confirmation of imperfection. There is safety in not deciding for lack of information or some other acceptable reason. One way to never make a poor decision is not to decide at all.

If you choose not to decide, you still have made a choice.
–Rush

Address this character quality as soon as possible and it will save you time, energy, and heartache. Perfection is not something to strive for, as it is forever unattainable. Instead, choose excellence as your North Star.

Haste Makes Waste

On the other side of the procrastination coin is the hasty decision maker. The popular mantra today of "fail fast, fail often" feeds this idea to combat perfectionism.

This method can be just as destructive as never deciding, because each decision will need to be integrated into the business. If a company is constantly adjusting to fresh changes, knowing if something isn't right will be difficult, because there is no baseline. Continual change can actually interfere with growth.

Making a decision without enough information is no better than taking too long to gather every piece of information possible. Sometimes, allowing an opportunity to pass by while determining if it is a good fit for the business is an acceptable course of action. The leader needs to balance how much time and input they need to make any decision. Sometimes haste really does make waste.

The Myth of First to Market

Another factor that can create decision time pressure is the concept of first to market. This cousin to "fail fast, fail often" encourages you to take your idea and push that product or service to market before your competition does. "Get an MVP (minimal viable product) to market," they say, usually followed by, "We'll iterate once it's out."

This pressure causes entrepreneurs to put products and services into the market before they are the best they can be (at least in their current version). First to market comes from a mindset of scarcity and following it as law creates unnecessary pressure for the entrepreneur.

I want to remind you: the iPod was not the first personal music device to fit in a person's pocket. There was no lack in excitement for the product when it arrived, even by those who owned other types. Nor was the iPhone the first mobile phone. There are countless examples of companies who were not first to market, yet ended up with major market share.

Do not fall prey to the siren song of first to market; instead focus on being best in class. Your market will appreciate the time you take to create and deliver a well-thought-out product or service and they'll appreciate upgrades that enhance it, rather than core features you didn't have time to include.

Pivot or Pitch

In the world of entrepreneurship, one decision holds tremendous conflict: the decision to pivot or pitch.

In the life cycle of their company, every entrepreneur faces the situation when a product or service falls flat and doesn't meet expectations. In those circumstances, you'll need to decide if you must completely rework, iterate, or improve your offering or just toss it out altogether.

There are many examples of entrepreneurs facing these dilemmas. Richard Branson has faced it in nearly every one of his ventures, from Virgin Airlines to Virgin Cola. The story of how Branson made the decision to challenge British Air's monopoly on UK airspace is an incredible example of courage and tenacity. For Virgin and Branson, it worked out in the end — but not without numerous challenges and decisions to press forward.

On the other side, few failures were more public than Virgin Cola. Branson's effort to take on the cola giant Coca-Cola forced him to re-evaluate what his product had to offer. By Branson's own admission, "We didn't follow our own rules, which is a cardinal sin. Virgin only enters an industry when we think we can offer consumers something strikingly different that will disrupt the market, but there wasn't really an opportunity to do that in the soft drinks sector."[3]

This "go or no go" is a crucial point for many businesses. If a product or service is a complete failure, we know it and the decision is easy: there is no path forward.

A more difficult point in an entrepreneur's life is when a product or service is not performing to expectation but isn't clearly a success or failure. What's the best road to take now? These are the circumstances — and the decisions — that try the souls of many entrepreneurs.

The decision to take a product or service to market is a bold one. The decision to pull a product or service from market can be even more difficult. Have methods and input you can rely on to guide you in these times. If you find yourself in this situation, always remember the touchstones of your vision and who you are serving.

Integrating Decision Results and Outcomes

Each decision has some degree of domino effect, whereby a change in one area of a company, product, or service will affect another. A company in constant change risks their ability to fully adopt one change before the next appears, and the time and energy to adapt affects their daily production.

When a leader is constantly "trying things out," their team can lose confidence that the leader has clear direction and vision. Your team must understand how any major decision plays into the vision of the company and how it affects their role.

I have seen first-hand the unrest within a company whose leader makes regular, sweeping changes. This culture of constant change is counterproductive. When a leader appears to lack focused direction, it confuses the team and disables their autonomy — due to lack of clear standards, role definitions, and expectations.

Another reorganization was in the works as I began working with Alex, the CEO. Alex had lots of exciting plans and was looking to better use his team's skills and increase productivity within the organization. This was why Alex called me in.

I wanted to understand all the pieces of the puzzle, so I asked, "Do you mind if I speak with the team individually so I can help you better with communication and leadership of this new structure you wish to implement with them?"

"Absolutely! That would help a lot. And maybe you can help me figure out how to get them excited about this," he replied, already convinced they just didn't like change.

I discovered that the team indeed didn't like change, but for a specific reason: this was the third time in the past year that Alex had come up with an idea to revamp the team's roles and responsibilities.

I quickly discovered that not only could none of the team members define for me exactly what their current role was, they were vague on what Alex expected of them for the new role he envisioned. Worse, they all felt resigned that if they made the effort to change, the new structure would only last a short time before they would have to change again. Reorganizations had become commonplace in the company and they felt it was more of a revolving door than a well-thought-out plan with clear objectives.

As one team member explained, "It's constantly 'let's try this and see if it works... Nope! Okay, let's try something else!'"

It was clear that the team didn't feel Alex had given them enough time to integrate the changes, and he'd not defined current role responsibilities before he presented them with new ones. This caused a great deal of anxiety, frustration, and a bunch of lost productivity and finger-pointing when things didn't get done well.

Being a founder is a lot like driving a car. The passengers may not even know where you are taking them, so it's important to recognize the trust they've placed in you. Even if they know where you hope to take them, they need to feel confident that you have thought over the route and will do everything possible to get them there safely. If you continually change the destination or threaten to "stop this car" it gives people a whole new distraction and sense of insecurity.

As you make changes to your organization or direction, think deeply about how this will affect others around you. Pay close attention to the needs of your team for information or stronger guidance to help them settle into any changes.

A team that feels that they have all the information behind changes and why those changes must be implemented will be stronger than those who feel in the dark. If you leave it to your team to answer their own questions, chances are good they guess wrong and that could derail your plans.

A constant state of change creates an atmosphere of uncertainty, with a corresponding negative impact on productivity and morale. Most humans do not flourish when uncertainty lasts for long periods. Avoid increasing the state of uncertainty in your company; entrepreneurial ventures hold such a high degree of this already.

Dealing with Decision Fatigue

It's estimated that the average adult makes about 35,000 remotely conscious decisions each day. Researchers at Cornell University estimate we make 219 decisions each day on food alone.[4] And as your level of responsibility increases, so does the multitude of choices you have to make. Building a business from scratch surely increases these numbers exponentially.

Even the most accomplished entrepreneurs will come to a point of exhaustion from the number of decisions they encounter. Over time, the weight of continually making important decisions causes fatigue, affecting the way we examine information and make decisions (if we have the energy to decide at all).

Decision fatigue is a studied phenomenon that can affect everyone – from the preschooler to the president. Experiencing decision fatigue is inevitable in our society, and more so as your responsibilities increase. The best method to manage it is to recognize, assess, and plan for it.

To manage the influence this fatigue can have on you, as a person and as an entrepreneur, your first step is to recognize and understand it. Decision fatigue results from having to process vast amounts of data, on choices that exceed a person's comfort and energy. Studies indicate this condition has many contributing factors, such as physical fatigue, blood sugar levels, and time of day. The good news here: we often can control those elements.

The level of fatigue varies from person to person and situation to situation, but once a person becomes fatigued, the quality of the decisions made suffers. The cognitive brain can only handle the processing of a finite amount of material before needing to be recharged. The amount of information each of us can process varies by: individual strengths, weaknesses, preferences, and comfort zone; volume and magnitude of responsibilities including decisions; the type of decisions and amount of risk involved; and the decision maker's current state of mind, nutrition, energy, and physical well-being.

Unfortunately, the solution is not simply to find the number of decisions you make well in a day and limit yourself to that number. The number and quality of decisions required, and your personal state are all variables that impact the onset and intensity of fatigue. Identifying these factors and how they affect you will be your best defense.

Decision fatigue is not evident all the time. The most self-aware person, for whom decision-making is their career, can suffer from decision fatigue without realizing their judgment is impaired.

In a famous study published by the National Academy of Sciences, psychologists researched judges making parole decisions.[5] These people are career decision makers, educated and trained to assess the data presented and make fair, consistent conclusions. And yet, the study highlights that even these skilled decision makers do not escape the effects of decision fatigue and its many ordinary contributing factors.

The study shows that parolees with identical circumstances had varying rates of success in obtaining parole based on the level of fatigue the judges experienced. It shows that unknowingly over time the judges would opt to delay making a decision, or deny parole, as factors of fatigue set in. As they tired, the judges would choose to not decide, avoiding the chance of a misjudgment that might cause greater harm because, in their minds, their ability to properly assess the criteria had been depleted.

You know this feeling I'm sure if sometimes by the end of the day you don't even want to decide what to eat for dinner. If judges fall prey to this condition, be assured that you, the entrepreneur, will, too.

Decision Fatigue Contributing Factors

Multiple factors create the conditions for decision fatigue, some of which we can manage. Knowing these factors allows us to recognize and possibly even control them.

The brain processes information at its greatest capability when fully rested. No matter the method you use to make decisions, being fully refreshed contributes to your ability to process information. This is one of the great many reasons that sleep is so important to the entrepreneur (more about sleep later!)

The brain needs to be in optimal form to process at its peak level, which means it needs the proper nutrition. In the parole judges study, the judges' glucose levels at various times of the day factored into their decision fatigue: results of the first case after lunch showed distinct differences than the results of the last case before lunch.

Stress has so many harmful effects on the entrepreneur, including impeding their ability to evaluate decisions. Stress taxes the same area of the brain that processes data — the prefrontal lobe — which causes decision fatigue at a rapid rate.

The impact technology has on decision fatigue is tremendous and rarely positive. The continual notifications we receive across the computer screen, phone, and tablet each hour create hundreds of micro-decisions we must make each day. This is a common but toxic environment for the entrepreneur. These hundreds of invisible decisions — which many don't even recognize they are making — all contribute to overall fatigue.

Understanding your peak state for decisions, and the factors that most commonly create decision fatigue in you, is a critical skill. You won't be able to make every decision in the peak state, and recognizing when you are not in the best state to make a decision gives you options: to improve your state, delay the decision, or seek support.

How Successful People Manage Decision Fatigue

There are many ways successful people deal with this very real dilemma of decision fatigue. While an entrepreneur cannot escape the need to make decisions, there are practices you can implement to put yourself in the best possible position.

Limit

Some successful people limit the number of decisions they make, avoiding any that hold little value to them. For example, Steve Jobs is famous for wearing his black turtleneck and jeans every day, or Mark Zuckerberg for his gray t-shirt and blue hoodie.

In a *Vanity Fair* interview, Barack Obama said, "I'm trying to pare down decisions. I don't want to make decisions about what I'm eating or wearing, because I have too many other decisions to make."[6]

In the same interview Obama states, "You need to focus your decision-making energy. You need to routinize yourself. You can't be going through the day distracted by trivia." Limiting insignificant choices eliminates the constant taxing of the decision-making brain, and can prevent or delay fatigue.

In every way they can, these uber-successful people reserve their energy for only the most important and meaningful decisions.

Schedule

Another tactic is to make as many routine decisions ahead of time as possible, such as choosing what to wear, when to exercise, and when to eat. Determining as many of the routine items in your weekly schedule as possible ahead of time reduces the need to decide daily. This is a habit that has many benefits and implementing it early on will serve you well.

Make decisions in your optimal state and capture them in your planner or calendar. Then simply follow your plan or schedule.

Delay

We live in a world of immediacy and often believe the illusion that all decisions need to be made as quickly as they arrive. This is more habit than reality. Take the time to determine if a decision is urgent or if you might put it off until you are in a more optimal state. Few decisions cannot wait 24 hours.

In my personal practice, before knowing any of the science behind decision fatigue, I implemented a 24-hour rule for my teenaged children. As a single mother working in the legal field, I was constantly in decision mode, which left me exhausted by the end of the workday.

At the time I had no idea what to call it, but I knew I was tired and not able to make the best or even fair decisions. So my default answer was no. Much like the judges in the study, no was a safer decision for me than to miss evaluating the information incorrectly.

Knowing that by the time I got home I could not make good assessments of my children's requests, I implemented a rule where they needed to give me 24-hour advance notice for any substantial request. This time allowed me to take in the request and "sleep on it" and reply the next day when I was better able to give my best decision. This is one example that the skills you implement as an entrepreneur are transferable to all areas of your life.

Do not confuse delay with avoidance. Deferring a decision until you are in a better state is not an excuse to avoid making an important decision. But do use this when you need it to be in the best state for an important decision.

Manage Distraction

One of the most effective ways to manage decision fatigue is to manage technology. There are many successful people who go to great lengths to give themselves uninterrupted time away from the demands of technology. The simple act of seeing a notification flash or even feeling your phone vibrate demands multiple decisions — and is terribly destructive for productivity.

The constant barrage of notifications is taxing to the processing capability of the brain. And the stress you feel as the needs of others regularly flash before you reduces your optimal state for important brain functioning.

Take technology breaks and shut down notifications when possible, even if only for short, concentrated amounts of time. When going into a meeting where you'll make important decisions, turn off or do not even bring your phone into the meeting to keep yourself in as prime mode as possible for the information you are receiving.

A vibrating phone is as much of a distraction as a visual notification. The best way to avoid depleting your resources is to turn it off or put it in another room, even if only for short periods when you need to concentrate.

Delegate

Delegation is not always possible, especially as an early stage entrepreneur. But consider using it when the opportunity arises. In the very beginning of a new venture, every decision — from paperclips to legal structure — needs to be made by the entrepreneur. This should be temporary.

As the company grows, your responsibilities grow with it, and you'll need to delegate to keep the volume manageable. Delegation of decisions requires a system, so the process doesn't create more decisions.

Delegation is a "front-end loaded" process, requiring a bit more time and energy at the beginning. Take time to create systems, explain process and expectations, and define levels of decisions, and you will reap the benefits over the long run. Make corrections or answer questions along the way to allow the person taking the work to have full understanding of the need and desired result. If the initial results are not perfect, make time to review the gaps and make adjustments.

From this early investment, you will free up your time for the things that only you can do.

Self-Assess

Self-assessment is a great tool to use each time you approach a major decision. There will be situations when you can take your time and get into an optimal state, and there will be times when that is not possible. Mitigate the known factors: have a snack while you consider, or take a ten-minute meditation or a 20-minute nap before coming to a full decision, to give yourself the best state for the situation.

Self-awareness is crucial as decision-maker to bring your best self to decisions that can have critical affects to the company. Managing the elements that affect and the number of decisions made will not prevent poor decisions, but it will minimize the possibility of not being able to take in data to make your best decision possible.

Decisions Are an Entrepreneurial Constant

In the end, you will make thousands of decisions as an entrepreneur. Doing the best you can with the information you have at the time and place of any decision is the most you can ask of yourself. Putting yourself in a prime state to assess and analyze each decision will give you the greatest opportunity for a positive outcome.

Decisions are one of the constants in an entrepreneur's life. Choose methods that will provide you the best way to analyze the data for any situation and control the factors you are able. Analyze failures and successes, then rinse and repeat.

In the end, know that you possess the tools to do the best you can. And know that most decisions are not life-and-death.

Decision-Making Exercises

Assessing Your Default Modes

- Which decision-making style do you most often default to?

- What factors or situations most often cause you to procrastinate?

- Do you consider yourself a perfectionist? What lies behind your need to be or do something perfectly?

Your Peak Decision-Making State:

- Do you have a time of day that you feel making decisions comes easier for you?

- Based on your past experiences, what factors play into your ability to make decisions that you feel good about?

- What factors do you feel personally affect your focus and ability to objectively process information for a peak-decision state?

Part 2

You Are Not an Island

CHAPTER 7

Empathy

If you want to build a business that lasts, employ empathy first.
–Elizabeth Miner

In this chapter:
- The value of empathy in your brand.
- Practicing empathy in the workplace.
- Vendor relationships beyond the contract.

Empathy is having its day in the sun in the world of leadership, and for good reason. It's the winning wildcard of a successful entrepreneur.

Empathy is the ability to put yourself in another's shoes and view a situation, product, or experience from their point of view. It requires curiosity and the intention to understand before responding or solving.

While empathy is not hard to cultivate, it does require attention and effort, particularly with the pace of the world today. But overlooking empathy can erode customer and employee loyalty and trust and cause long-term brand damage.

We have seen countless companies fall from grace when their CEOs give tone-deaf responses to sensitive situations and flagrantly disregard the feelings or values of their employees and customers.

Let's look at the United Airline's Teflon-coated response to a worldwide public relations nightmare after forcibly removing a passenger from their flight. The CEO's statement about how the company handled the situation lacked any empathy for the feelings of those on the initial flight and heightened fears for any future passengers that purchased tickets were potentially retractable.

According to reports, on April 9, 2017, after passengers were seated in the United Express Flight 3411 and still at the gate, a United gate agent announced that four passengers would need to be removed, in order to accommodate four staff members who had to cover an unstaffed flight at another location.

The reports go on to describe through account witnesses that a passenger was requested to relinquish his seat but politely refused. In an effort to enforce the removal of the passenger, the airport security officers were called to physically remove the passenger. This situation escalated whereby the passenger was injured and video footage from other passengers was distributed showcasing the poor treatment of the passenger.

Later that day, United issued a statement: "Flight 3411 from Chicago to Louisville was overbooked. After our team looked for volunteers, one customer refused to leave the aircraft voluntarily and law enforcement was asked to come to the gate. We apologize for the overbook situation. Further details on the removed customer should be directed to authorities."

United CEO Oscar Munoz stated on April 10: "This is an upsetting event to all of us here at United. I apologize for having to re-accommodate these customers. Our team is moving with a sense of urgency to work with the authorities and conduct our own detailed review of what happened. We are also reaching out to this passenger to talk directly to him and further address and resolve this situation."

Later on April 10, in an e-mail to employees that appeared in the press, Munoz praised and defended the crew's actions, while claiming the passenger was "disruptive and belligerent." He stated that "Our employees followed established procedures for dealing with situations like this."

In a subsequent public statement released by United on the afternoon of April 11, 2017, Munoz was more conciliatory. His note described the incident as "truly horrific" and expressed an understanding of the "outrage, anger, disap-

pointment" felt by many. He took full responsibility and apologized, stating "No one should ever be mistreated this way." He promised to conduct a thorough review and release a report by April 30. The public statement ends with "I promise you we will do better."

Consider also the number of companies, like Uber and Facebook, that have poorly responded to gender bias and pay discrimination issues. The list goes on — and it's not a list you or your company want to be on.

When we integrate empathy into the culture of an organization, the business, employees, and clients all benefit. We will look at companies like Patagonia, Virgin, and eBay as examples of how exhibiting empathy and connecting with their customers has added to their brand loyalty.

What Empathy Looks Like

As an entrepreneur, you need empathy in multiple areas of your business, and empathy looks different in each one. For the customer or client, empathy will come across in your customer service, product design, and sometimes even your sourcing. With your clients, empathy shows in the way they feel cared for by your business.

As the CEO of your business, use empathy in how you engage with your team and any staff to secure productivity, build loyalty, create value, and save yourself expensive turnover. This form of empathy centers on the effort to notice the why behind the what. As Simon Sinek explains, when your top-performing salesperson begins underperforming, the conversation to be had is one of empathy, not discipline.

Even in working with vendors, empathy is an often-undisclosed currency benefitting all. Understanding the needs of your vendors and suppliers encourages better negotiations, where parties form a partnership to produce extensive benefits for both. Sourcing in a way that speaks to your business's and customer's values, with awareness of how you obtain materials and provide services, is how empathy shows up in your brand identity.

In each of the following sections we'll break down each of these three areas where the entrepreneur's skill with empathy can make a significant difference to their business.

Customer Empathy

Your customer is the heart of your business. Let's face it — without them, you have nothing but a great idea.

Customers are more than just numbers and currency signs; they are the humans that give your business purpose and the people who spend money keeping you in business. To acknowledge your clients as individuals sounds easy and obvious, but one only needs to go into any marketing meeting to begin to lose perspective.

Avatars and *target markets* all represent humans who purchase your products or services. Without care and attention, these processes may allow the personal element to slip from focus. This is a slippery slope where empathy diminishes, and dehumanization begins.

One thing Richard Branson is known for is his focus on the people he works with. He believes the ideas of both employees and customers hold so much information about how the company is doing and what might be improved, that he takes the opportunity every time he flies his airline, Virgin, to speak with them.

Reportedly Branson walks through the plane to ask customers and staff about their experience, taking notes in his famous notebook. Branson runs billions of dollars of businesses and in his opinion, no detail is too small. He asks the people closest to the product about their experience.

"It's the little things," he says, that often make the biggest difference. "Letting people be heard; everyone has an opinion, so listen." Listening to everyone when he can connect directly with staff and customers makes them feel appreciated and cared for. Implementing ideas that have come from those conversations creates loyalty no money can buy.

One of the major ways to ensure loyalty is to make your customers feel you care about them, their problem that your product or service addresses, and their happiness with their experience. While you can attempt to put yourself in your client's shoes, it benefits you to actually do it (give your product or service a test run), or speak directly with customers and get their honest feedback.

Clients who feel a brand or business truly cares about their needs and satisfaction develop a loyalty that surpasses price. Not only does this create a secure customer base; but these customers become an integral part of your marketing team — a ready source of testimonials, word-of-mouth advertising (the best kind), and referrals. You create raving fans with great products and services that meet the client's needs, and empathetic business practices that show you care.

There is no better example from modern-day marketing that I can think of than Patagonia.

In 2011 on Black Friday, Patagonia ran this full-page ad in *The New York Times*:

DON'T BUY
THIS JACKET

Photo by Tim Nudd on Adweek [7]

Patagonia has built its brand on the value of environmental responsibility and in their industry, like many, they face challenges to balance that responsibility with profitability. The company has made significant efforts to be bold in their vision and creative in their solutions. Though they never claim to be 100% sustainable, they are transparent about where they stand and what they are doing to move closer to that goal.

Environmental sustainability is a large part of what resonates with their consumer base: outdoor enthusiasts who have a need for quality and a strong desire to do minimal harm to the earth.

The brilliance of the ad is this: it put the company's mission first and sales second. No one reading it could question what this company was about, and the ad raised awareness for some who may not have understood the story behind the Patagonia brand.

The ad did not shame anyone for wanting a new coat, but instead provided options for the customer to feel better about their purchase if they made one. It gave the customer a variety of ways to feel aligned with something bigger, to address a problem they want to be part of solving.

This is an outstanding example of brand empathy. Patagonia clearly put themselves in the shoes (or coats) of their consumer and asked, "What can we do to help people feel good about buying a new item for themselves?" They also solved the problem of "What options can we provide to help the article they are replacing continue to be in use for another person and thereby increase sustainability?"

Connecting with your customer defines your market clearly and provides options for a bigger impact when you unite with them under a common goal or value.

Workplace Empathy

Empowering others to succeed requires psychological safety.
–Sundar Pichai, CEO Google/Alphabet

> *Boss: Angela, you're late again. This is the third time this week.*
>
> *Angela: Yes, it won't happen again.*
>
> *Boss, without empathy: If it continues, we may have to let you go. You need to be here on time; it affects other people and critical processes.*
>
> *Boss, with empathy: Angela, this isn't like you. Is there something going on that we can help with?*

Is Angela having trouble at home? Is there a change in her home routine that affects her ability to meet the timing she originally agreed to? Is Angela losing interest in work? Is there something going on at work that is causing her not to want to be there?

There are so many questions and possibilities for why Angela may not be getting to work on time. Yes, you can demand she be prompt, but in doing so you miss the opportunity to learn more, maybe even about something in the office you should know.

By beginning with empathy, you create the opportunity to learn about Angela's needs instead of simply dictating your own. Maybe you can't help directly, but simply by asking, you have shown you care about her as a person, which can lead to a deeper relationship.

Leading with empathy can create a more supportive environment, more open communication, and deeper connection between the people involved. Giving someone the opportunity to share their situation does not mean you need to solve it, but it gives you more information to see what is behind the behavior.

Angela: Actually, my partner's been sick, and I have had to get the children ready for daycare and school this week and it's gotten me behind each morning. I'm sorry, I'll try to get here on time.

Boss, with empathy: Wow, that must be stressful for all of you. Let's ask the team if someone can cover your morning responsibilities this week or until your routine can get back to normal. Would that be helpful?

Empathy requires you to look beyond the obvious. It requires you to suspend judgment and ask questions. As someone under a lot of pressure and stress, this may not be the easiest of your EQ skills to employ, but approaching situations with curiosity first will foster a culture of connection and compassion.

Empathy takes courage to imagine yourself in the experience of another. This is not to pity someone or show sympathy, which creates distance. Empathy instead encourages you to feel another's experience, which invites connection.

As the leader of a group of people, your empathy creates such a powerful space. Empathy from a leader will draw people together in solidarity and helps to create cohesive teams. Sympathy, on the other hand, creates a gap between the people involved and can lead to people feeling less than others because of their situation.

Brené Brown, a leading researcher of vulnerability and empathy, explains empathy as the ability to see the world/experience/situation someone is sharing through their eyes, setting aside your own perception of what it may be. Something that might not be a big deal to you may weigh heavily on someone else; curiosity is necessary here.

A person in pain or conflict sharing something that is affecting them takes vulnerability. As a leader, or even as someone who is part of a community with this person, the ability to provide empathy has so many positive effects. Empathy, especially in the role of leadership, provides a united feeling that whatever someone may be facing, they are not alone and by their sharing the situation they have support.

In the workplace this requires several things to be in place:

- A space where people feel valued and safe is the foundational requirement.

- Autonomy within the organization, which fosters the ability to problem solve within a team for the benefit of its members and the business.

- A culture that values and encourages empathy, which builds trust and loyalty.

This base serves a company well, by decreasing turn-over, fostering team accountability, and enhancing the ability to recruit top talent.

Studies show that people desire to work in a company where they feel they make a difference and feel valued. These two factors *beat salary and benefits* in studies on employee retention.

Build a company where people feel valued and connected to each other and you will have one less hurdle to manage. People are the foundation of every company. Make it your priority to cultivate a culture of empathy to support the heartbeat of your business.

Vendor Empathy

Vendor empathy is rarely written about, but it is an important facet of empathy to consider, particularly for new entrepreneurs. As a new business owner, you may not have the volume or financial leverage that other businesses your vendors deal with may have — so empathy may be the biggest offering you have.

Let's face it: empathy is all about relationships and one of the most important relationships you will have is with your vendors and suppliers. Build these relationships strong for the benefit of both parties and everyone wins.

The most obvious place vendor empathy shows up is in negotiations. Working contracts so there are benefits for both parties is one pure form of empathy. This does not mean that you do not negotiate for your position, but that you see each negotiation from both sides, so that everyone wins in the end.

Richard Branson spends a lot of time understanding what the person on the other side of the table wants. Once he knows this, he can consider what he is willing to sacrifice to benefit the other and encourage the same from the other person.

Do not assume that both parties are battling for the same thing; take the time to ask questions and listen so you can understand and craft a resolution where everyone gains what is most important to them. If this is not entirely possible, it might be best to walk away to preserve the relationship for a future situation or need.

Practicing empathy with your vendors sets the stage for future positive negotiations. It also provides a strong base during times of shortages or unforeseen circumstances. Having good relationships with your vendors makes a difference in how they may be able to provide services or resources.

One only needs to look at the recent situation of the pandemic of 2020. The effects of COVID disrupted supply chains around the globe and forced services and businesses to make drastic changes. Customers around the world found new ways to support businesses they valued. Vendors and suppliers worked with businesses in creative ways to help their key customers survive the challenges they were facing. What an amazing display of empathy in action!

All around the world, COVID and its fallout disrupted life as we knew it in a way no contracts could account for. It was the relationships businesses formed that determined if they thrived or even survived these challenges. Individuals chose to sacrifice a little to maintain the business, whether as a team member, customer, or a vendor.

This time in history was the largest show of empathy in business in my lifetime. If you think that your relationship with your vendors is not critical once you sign the contract or serve your customer their product, you would have learned differently in 2020.

Employ Empathy for the Good of Your Relationships and Your Business

Empathy takes effort and intention. As an entrepreneur, you'll need to take extra time implementing this skill into all your interpersonal transactions and building your culture. You may need to train yourself to respond in a way you haven't practiced and teach others to apply this skill to realize its full benefits.

Mastering and incorporating the elements of perspective, avoiding judgment, emotional awareness, open conversation, and collaborative problem-solving in your leadership is the groundwork of a positive culture. A positive culture will reach far beyond the business walls and your efforts will be rewarded.

The benefits of empathy in business cross over every aspect with a human element (meaning all of them). Take care of the people who work for you and with you as individuals apart from the business and you will generate solidarity and loyalty.

Bake empathy into the customer journey and receive the reward of free marketing from your valued customers.

Ensure your vendor relationships are ones of partnership not adversary and you will benefit from the non-tangible resource of goodwill that will be there if you ever need to call on it.

Empathy is good for business in every way. Take the time to develop this skill and practice it in every human interaction you have as an entrepreneur and you will reduce your chances of becoming one more business failure statistic.

Empathy Exercises

- Make a list of the concerns, initiatives, and views of your target customer to see where there is an intersection with a product or service your company provides. (The best place to get this information? Your potential or current customer! Ask them.)

- Consider programs or initiatives that support your team members to expand their sense of belonging and connection within the company and team.

- Review your vendor and suppliers looking beyond the financial interaction for opportunities to enhance your connection with their company mission or initiatives.

CHAPTER 8

Leadership

In this chapter:
- Building key leadership attributes through emotional intelligence.
- Self-awareness for effective leadership.
- Taking care of those in your charge versus being in charge.

More than 200 years ago, a man in civilian clothes came upon a small group of tired and battle-weary soldiers. They were digging what appeared to be an important defensive position.

The leader of the group wasn't making any effort to help. He just shouted orders and threatened to punish the group if the work wasn't completed within the hour.

"Why aren't you helping?" asked the stranger on horseback.

"I'm in charge! The men do as I tell them," said the leader. He added, "Help them yourself if you feel so strongly about it."

To the leader's surprise, the stranger got off his horse and helped the men until they finished the job. Before he left, the stranger congratulated the men for their work, and approached the confused leader.

"You should notify top command next time your rank prevents you from supporting your men — and I will provide a more permanent solution," the stranger said. Up close, the now-humbled leader recognized General George Washington — and received a lesson he would never forget!

Leader Is Not a Title

Many people who call themselves leaders or influencers do not possess the skills, tools, or mindset to genuinely be what they call themselves. There is a clear difference between authority and leadership; this chapter will address that distinction. Let me be clear from the outset: leader is not a title; it is a way of being.

When we think of the great leaders over the years, they have certain similar qualities. Most leaders are born through difficult experiences, which tested their ethics, morality, and grit. Leadership is not something given because of longevity in the field, you earn it through the experiences people have with you.

When we think of poor leaders, we think of those who have put themselves and their desires ahead of others. They blame others for failures and take credit for successes that aren't theirs. They are not revered for their leadership but followed out of fear of their power.

The ability to become a leader is open to all — at any time, at any level.

At the core of every effective and revered leader is an emotionally intelligent person. Someone secure enough in their abilities and knowledge to be open to differing information. Someone willing to make tough decisions. Someone who takes responsibility for failures and shares credit when things go well.

Those who possess the traits and characteristics of a great leader earned the title through repeated actions that built trust among those who follow them. These people become leaders because they inspire others by their purpose, and by the sense of safety and security they create for those around them.

The role of the entrepreneur contains many leadership opportunities — regardless of the size of the venture. Even the act of stepping out as an entrepreneur uses many leadership skills.

We've all experienced that feeling when we know we're in the presence of a good leader. (Just as we've all experienced the opposite: when someone held the title, but hadn't earned it.) Here we will break down what elements create those feelings and set apart the powerful leader from the ineffective one.

We typically find the following traits in powerful leaders, but their use determines positive or negative impact.

Strategic Thinking

As an entrepreneur, combining the roles of dreamer and planner is essential. It is also necessary to decide and direct how to move the big picture of the vision forward.

Building a strategy that brings a vision into reality is one of the critical leadership roles of an entrepreneur.

It is important in this role to be positive and optimistic — but not blindly so. Throughout the life cycle of the company, you'll need those skills you developed to bring your unproven vision forward. Being aware of bias and ensuring diverse input will strengthen your ability to see potential challenges. (More on Bias and Diversity in the next chapter.)

In a *Harvard Business Review* article, research conducted by the Wharton School[8] identified the skills essential to strategic leadership. According to the study, the area where many leaders fail is in anticipating the market and preparing for changes.

More important than leading in a crisis is the ability to predict and prevent one. Without strategy to drive the business, you leave success to chance, versus making calculated risks and defining goals. As much as you drive the daily progress, you must also strategically prepare for what you and your company will need in the future.

Forecasting future needs for continual growth is challenging in the unpredictable and dynamic world of entrepreneurship. You need an eye towards the future and your feet in the present to lead the company strategically to its ultimate vision.

The tale of Kodak shows what can happen when companies cannot shift their strategic plan as the market turns:

> In 1975, a Kodak engineer invented the first digital camera. Many stories claim Kodak ignored this new field, which led to their demise — but a deeper look says this was not the case.

Kodak did pursue and benefit from the digital camera market for some time; however, the advent of digital cameras destroyed their most lucrative business model: film developing, and Kodak did not adapt their core business to the change.

Their position as first in market created the opportunity to anticipate what others did not yet see. Unfortunately, they failed to implement strategic planning for this market turn and ultimately destroyed their core business model without a replacement as product needs shifted.

Technology allows markets to change rapidly and adapting to the changes in your industry is critical to your longevity. Relying heavily on any single portion of your business is not wise, and strategic planning for how things will change is both a necessary and difficult challenge. The catalyst for the destruction of your primary revenue source may even come from within, as it did with Kodak, so being on top of strategic partnerships and pivoting business models is a constant need.

Keeping your finger on the pulse of your industry, participating in its growth, and positioning your company for success are all important aspects of strategic leadership. Being self-aware will help keep your eyes open to possibilities for your market — both positive and negative.

Strategy creates the confidence that surprises will be minimal. As a strong leader, you will want to excel in this area. Having a mentor here can accelerate your progress.

Vision

Good business leaders create a vision, articulate the vision, passionately own the vision, and relentlessly drive it to completion.
–Jack Welch

To be a leader you must possess a strong, clear vision of what you want to accomplish. From Henry Ford to Steve Jobs and everyone in between, influential leaders have a view of what might be and inspire others to join them in turning their vision into reality.

A vision of a positive future compels the entrepreneur. This quality is inherent in them and being visionary is usually something that permeates all areas of their life.

Having any vision is not enough; the quality of the vision is also extremely important.

Simon Sinek calls this quality vision a *just cause* — where the full expression of the vision may not be realized in one lifetime, but the *cause* will continually move forward. Those who pursue such a cause will accept the effort and sacrifices necessary to advance the ultimate vision and fulfill this meaningful goal.

Leaders with visions that promote only personal gain can be equally compelling — for a time. But those who lead for personal gain or lead through fear of retribution ultimately destroy the following they've created. Followers of such a vision will eventually recognize and expose the selfishness of that goal and reject the leadership they willingly granted.

A vision may be the impetus, but leadership begins when you can communicate your vision clearly and compellingly, and connect it with the wants and needs of others.

Simplicity

Hand in hand with having a meaningful vision is the ability to share it. The goals of the vision and the company and anything being done by a leader rely on other people being able to connect to it.

Richard Branson says, "Complexity is your enemy. Any fool can make something complicated. It is hard to make something simple."

Complexity does not show intelligence or value. Simplifying a complex issue is often difficult but it opens the field for more people to get behind an idea. The more others understand the idea, the better opportunity there is for sharing and adopting the new concept.

An example of simplicity at work: Steve Jobs felt that Bill Gates's vision "to have a computer in every household" could not advance without simplifying the product. Jobs took the complexity out of using computers and MS-DOS systems[9] to meet the needs of the public.

By creating a user interface and user experience that people could use without reading pages of directions or learning a new language, Jobs and Apple met the consumer where they were, and propelled Apple's rise. By taking complexity out of the product. Apple expanded its already potent vision to meet the needs of a larger user base.

Vision is limited without the ability to engage others. Without clarity and simplicity, a brilliant idea may never reach those it can affect, and instead will die alone.

Communication Skills

The best leaders will clearly articulate their vision in a way that engages and inspires others to follow.

More than just speaking or writing well, an influential leader must possess the skills to communicate clearly to share needed information. True communication transfers important information in a way that one's audience can receive it.

So often people speak to share their ideas and then wonder why they are not getting the results they desire. Talking and communicating are as different as hearing and listening are. Emotional intelligence plays a big role here, as those who are empathetic are better able to assess their audience to deliver a clear message.

A skilled leader adapts the method of sharing information to their audience. If we want to be heard and understood, we need to present information to others in a way that they can understand it.

When I conduct events, I use a simple example to highlight the real disconnect between those giving and receiving information. The funniest example comes directly from my own learning experience.

One day, immediately before beginning an exercise with two executives, one of them explained to me he had to leave in ten minutes. This wasn't a lengthy exercise, so I assured him we'd complete his portion in that time. I hurriedly gave the instructions and as we began, the whole exercise went in a completely different direction from what I intended.

This was an incredible lesson for me: of providing a clear framework to produce desired results. I know that when I rush, I often make assumptions and often eliminate time for questions. I should not find it a surprise that in these instances I fail to produce the results I expect.

When the executive with the time commitment left, I repeated the activity, but much less rushed this time. I had experienced how both executives interpreted my instructions and I could be specific and clear. The results were starkly different. Knowing how the remaining executive heard me and taking time to explain the exercise in a way this person could understand produced the ultimate success.

What a helpful reminder for me! I thoroughly recognized this pattern in myself, yet because of the time pressure, I neglected to change my plan. I did not acknowledge the situation and reschedule the exercise, but I opted to rush it instead, which produced sub-optimal results.

If you think about some of the great ideas of our time, the speaker relayed them in plain talk in a way the audience could relate. Think of Martin Luther King, Jr., and his "I Have a Dream" speech. Think about John F. Kennedy and his idea of putting men on the moon. Both men had their audience in mind; they didn't speak in grandiose terms using legal or technical jargon.

These inspiring leaders used stories to convey bold visions in complex areas of law and aerospace. They communicated these ideas in ways people could get behind, with stories they could relate to, and with language they could use to share what they learned with others.

Thinking about how your audience might explain what you just told them is a great way to choose your language. As an entrepreneur, it is critical you make communication skills a priority.

Matching Communication Styles

You would not communicate to an audience in a language they don't understand, but most times that is exactly what happens — even when we use the same dialect.

When you draw a picture for someone whose learning style is verbal or written, you lose so much of the message. Likewise, if someone learns by interacting physically with the process, drawing pictures might be close, but actively engaging this type of learner will be most helpful.

Although we write millions of emails and texts every day, true communication is at an all-time low. Technology advances provide us additional methods to deliver information quickly, but they rarely address that each person consumes information differently.

In the fast pace of today's world, people shoot off emails to get tasks off their list without considering the recipient and their ability to receive the information in the way intended. There is so much miscommunication in our communication because people have lost the art in the rush.

We are not so far into the technological age that we can download information directly into another's brain — so we need to work with the human interface present. Although taking this time may feel like the longer route, it's the more effective one, and likely will save time overall.

For entrepreneurs, communication in all forms is critical to success. This is an area you must master; you cannot overlook it nor hand it off. To be an effective leader, you must skillfully assess how people receive information and communicate in a way that connects with them, while minimizing conflicts of understanding.

Empathy

We spent an entire chapter on empathy already, so I won't get too detailed here, but empathy is an integral trait in great leadership. Simon Sinek, who has studied leaders from the military to corporations, repeatedly states that the role of the leader "is not about being in charge. Leadership is about taking care of those in your charge."

Great leadership recognizes the humanness of those under their direction. Acknowledging that people have many elements that play into how they show up to work can mean the difference between a disengaged worker and a superstar performer.

Having empathy as a leader is speaking to the whole person. Being interested in the human being benefits them, benefits you, and benefits your company.

Integrity

The supreme quality for leadership is unquestionably integrity. Without it, no real success is possible, no matter whether it is on a section gang, a football field, in an army, or in an office.
–Dwight D. Eisenhower

It should be without question that leaders exhibit integrity. When we discover someone isn't leading with integrity — like Elizabeth Holmes of Theranos or the "leadership" at Enron — it feels like a personal betrayal.

A leader without integrity will eventually lose the trust of those who believed in them and, ultimately, they will lose all power. The fall from leadership in these instances often comes at a significant cost, both personal and professional.

Leadership is a responsibility. Integrity is not being infallible; it is being honest in challenging times and acting with moral principles even when no one is looking. It is an unfair ideal to believe that we'll make no errors, so when issues do inevitably arise, the best scenario is full transparency. In this way, integrity goes hand in hand with building confidence.

A bond of trust between leaders and followers is important and, once broken, is difficult to rebuild.

We will not explore the leagues of leaders without integrity (the nightly news takes care of that). Here instead we'll outline what integrity in leadership looks like.

Do What You Say You're Going to Do

This is such a simple statement, and synonymous with integrity. Words without action are fruitless and create uncertainty. To be a person of your word builds trust and confidence, which are the backbones of leadership.

A leader that keeps their word provides a certainty and a level of safety that others can rely on. This is such an integral piece of trust-building and must be front of mind any time you make a commitment.

Values

Being a person of integrity means living one's values and placing those above all else. The best leaders are those people can trust to always be true and consistent to their values, regardless of the situation.

A leader's values show up in how they act and how they treat people. Outlining your core values, those of your company, or even of a particular role, is necessary for others to have a clear understanding and ability to align with your cause and your leadership.

Standards

People have high standards for their leaders. They see traits and characteristics in a leader that they like and would like to embody within themselves.

Having high standards for yourself as a leader and continually working to live them is a great responsibility and challenge. But do not confuse high standards with needing to be superhuman.

Living up to high expectations as a leader is a great motivator, because you must measure each action against an ideal. Being conscious of your standards and expectations encourages you to create the highest-level product or service as a representation of these standards.

Those who have come to rely on the leader's standards can develop a deep trust that they will only put forth a certain quality of work. This expectation as a leader will set the tone for all dealings and pay dividends.

Learn to Earn Your Leadership

Leadership is not just about making decisions; it is maintaining the course as distractions appear.

This trait again creates trust in the unwavering concentration of the leader to advance their vision. The leader pushes ahead, acting as a guide for others to rely upon. This operational and emotional role requires emotional intelligence.

Leadership is a role you will learn and earn. As you move through this journey, your leadership skills will grow and improve. You will not get everything right, but how you lead when you don't — and during times of turmoil — will be an important part of what builds your skill.

Leadership Exercises
Leadership Style

- Think about a leader you admire. What leadership traits do you feel that person possesses that you'd like to emulate? What leadership traits do they have that you already possess?

- Consider your leadership style. What is one thing you might change or enhance to take better care of those you lead?

Communication Style

- Think about your own communication/learning style — do you learn best by doing, pictures, text, or talking?

- How do you usually communicate your ideas with others? How could you incorporate other communication/learning styles into your communications?

CHAPTER 9

Bias & Diversity

In this chapter:

- Recognizing bias in you.
- Making diversity and inclusion work for everyone.
- Developing your company culture.

In 2020, the Black Lives Matter movement reawakened across the US and globally, highlighting the many areas of inequity in our world and bringing needed attention to the related concepts of racism, prejudice, and bias.

In this chapter, we'll discuss how bias can show up in your life and business, and how emotional intelligence can help understand bias. We'll also cover how embracing a culture of diversity — or reversing a culture of bias against "others" and instead embracing them — are beneficial to your company and your business.

An entrepreneur can use diversity to their benefit and avoid the pitfalls of bias only if they recognize it. Our experiences shape what we notice, how we react, and ultimately how we treat those around us. These topics span not only race, gender, and culture — but all the ways people are different.

As a business leader you have a responsibility bigger than your company: to contribute positively to a world you wish to live in. Equally important is the responsibility to build your company intentionally around what you value. Finally, seeking diversity will ensure your products and services meet the entirety of your market.

Merriam-Webster's definition of bias:

a: an inclination of temperament or outlook especially: a personal and sometimes unreasoned judgment: PREJUDICE
b: an instance of such prejudice
c: BENT, TENDENCY
d(1): deviation of the expected value of a statistical estimate from the quantity it estimates
(2): systematic error introduced into sampling or testing by selecting or encouraging one outcome or answer over others.

Why do we talk about bias in entrepreneurship? Didn't we already cover it with self-awareness?

The answer is yes and no. Understanding our biases is a part of self-awareness, but the topic is complex, and important, and deserves specific, thoughtful attention. The importance of creating an entire chapter around bias is this: it can have an enormous impact on your business. It can affect who you do business with, who you hire, and the products and services you create.

How Did We Get Here?

First, let's look at the way we all develop biases — all humans have them, and some animals too! All bias isn't bad, but bias is not fact.

Bias grows out of our experiences, both conscious and unconscious. Biases are familial, religious, territorial, and societal — and some intertwine so deeply into our subconscious that we may not even notice them. Applying all facets of emotional intelligence will benefit our work on bias.

As children, we are born a blank slate. Our experiences and exposure write biases upon us.

TV shows you were exposed to may cast certain cultures or skin tones in a particular role. Books provided in school are usually from a majority-class author. The education system may portray the country providing education in the best light possible. There are so many ways we are unknowingly provided biased information; our mind begins to categorize people, places, and things without explicit instruction.

To say that bias is not your fault is an understatement. Because of your exposure to biased material from your earliest days, you may not even be aware of your biases or where they come from. What is in your control is how you address it once you have awareness. It is your responsibility to examine this, as a member of our shared humanity.

Many Faces

As you go about your days, you may or may not recognize thoughts that pass through your mind; but once you become aware, you cannot ignore them. I encourage you to pay special attention to thoughts about those you pass when walking down the street, in a market, or as you go about your day.

How you greet the receptionist at the doctor's office — as well as the nurse and the doctor — is a prime opportunity for this awareness. Recognize your assumptions, question them, and address any you find that show bias or don't serve you: do you assume all females are nurses? Or all males are doctors? What about receptionists? Do you have assumptions about their education?

In this one visit you may recognize some very subtle but noticeable differences in your thoughts about each person, based only on their role, without knowing anything more specific about the individual. This is one example of bias. This and other biases may be based on speech, education, appearance, gender, age, nationality, or any visible factor.

Your mind is always categorizing people, and while it is deciding if they are safe/not safe, friendly/hostile, your mind may develop immediate thoughts about someone — without any reason you're aware of. Pausing and developing this awareness will open the door to intentionality.

Awareness Is Step One

You cannot create for a world you do not yet see. When developing your target market, you may miss a huge sector simply by having an undiscovered bias.

Not having a full understanding of the world around you is what creates blind spots. For example: is your physical product labeled in brail? If you offer communication opportunities with your business, do you have non-audio options for your hearing-impaired customers? Is your physical storefront accessible to anyone with a physical handicap? Is your website using a font and contrast designed to be read easily by the visually impaired?

This goes beyond the actual company and into every item that represents your company. Does the content on your printed materials have enough contrast for visually impaired people? Is the font size small or a difficult typeface? Consider even that today's children are not learning to write or read script — so anything in that font might eliminate a whole generation of potential customers from understanding your product!

These questions often go overlooked based on your personal experiences. If you or someone you know is not vision or hearing impaired, would you even remember to make your company available to them? Although you did not intentionally omit these customers, by not addressing their specific needs, they don't feel welcomed, and worse, must make extra effort to use your products or services.

Is there additional expense in time, money, and energy here? Yes. Is it part of your mission or value for your company to be inclusive and accessible? This is not about a niche market; this is about the human market, which comes in all variations.

How Do We Ensure Against Our Bias?

Being self-aware and educating yourself is always a good start to exploring biases you may not have been aware of in yourself. Question everything: all your thoughts and feelings as they come up. You won't eradicate all your biases by yourself; I encourage you to take additional steps to expand your point of view.

Bias grows out of your experiences and point of view, so to take in new information effectively you need to engage others with different experiences. You may not notice something you are doing is not inclusive, because you've only experienced it from your own perspective. It is impossible to empathize with experiences you are unaware of.

Bring in someone whose background differs from yours and you learn about the way others might perceive something. Seeking out diverse individuals (with their unique ideas, observations, experiences, and points of view) and asking for input is critical to making the once-invisible visible.

Having diversity around you is the key to being inclusive and creating products and services that are truly accessible to the entire market you wish to serve. Include diverse perspectives on your team, your focus groups, and your board of directors and your business will benefit.

Bringing diversity in all levels of your business is the best way to account for your diverse market. Think of your internal team as a reflection of your customer base.

Bringing in different perspectives and experiences is not enough by itself. You must also create an environment and culture that supports different views, and encourages and respects input that differs from your own or the majority you belong to. Diversity is an empty initiative without inclusivity.

In Practice

It is important for business owners to have clear expectations about inclusive language and behaviors that celebrate diversity and provide team members ease of expression within the business. Saying everyone is welcome, and creating an environment where everyone feels equally valued, are two very different things.

This is not about being politically correct or washing out anything that "could" be construed as non-inclusive. It is celebrating all and giving the same weight to the impact and feedback of each individual.

Setting language expectations of respect cannot be overlooked. Don't assume that everyone understands how to address each other respectfully, because the world is continually evolving and more complex than it once was.

From how we regard each person as an individual to how we respect each role, we can address all of these by being thoughtful with language. This effort and distinction becomes part of the DNA of the culture of your business.

When people feel safe to express themselves, knowing they have respect, they will offer benefits to the business that would otherwise have been lost to fear. When we celebrate people for thinking differently, we open ourselves to opportunities for an array of innovation and contribution.

The Power of Questions

Bias may have been present in your original business concept, design, or creation of your product or service — simply because it filled a specific need or solved a specific problem. Initially that is not an issue; it's part of the process. But once you've gone beyond the initial phase of creation is where you need to question, recognize, and address any bias that's present.

Now is the time to bring diversity into the picture. When you take an idea and begin to mold it, questions are key to identifying biases and increasing accessibility. Creating and understanding your target market is where you will gain the most benefit from diverse perspectives.

Once you've asked the general questions: "Who would benefit from this product or service?" and, "How would they benefit?" — I suggest you dig deeper and ask, "How can I make my product or service more inclusive?" "Is there a group or classification that this product or service does not serve and why?"

Having a narrow target market is important, particularly to start, so you can focus on serving them well. No matter your target group, it will have variations. For example, if your target market is women ages 30–40, are you accounting for Trans, Black, Latina, Asian, or physically disabled women, too — and how their needs and perspectives might differ?

Your products/services may not serve some segments of a market, by choice or by oversight. Do those groups not have the same problem to solve? Or did you just overlook their specific needs? Is your marketing inclusive, both in the language and images it uses, and in the way it's presented? Does your client/customer see themselves in your advertising, fit in your product, or have access to it?

Finally, I encourage you to explore beyond who *does* my product/ service serve, and consider who *could* my product/service serve?

Dangerous Market Oversight

The modern automobile industry contains a blatant example of market oversight.

Even though statistics today show a near equal percentage of male and female drivers, the automobile industry has historically designed cars around "the average male," not considering at all the needs of female customers. Most cars designed around the "average male" driver overlook things like ease of reach for controls, positioning and fit of seatbelts, and seat sizes for smaller or larger drivers, ignoring the needs of those who don't fit the "standard."

This "average male" bias created more serious concerns than comfort and function: this bias affected vehicle safety as well.

Car companies first introduced crash-test dummies in the 1950s, built around an "average" male at the time — height, weight, muscle-mass proportions, and skeletal configurations — all vastly different than those of females. It wasn't until 2011 that the US began using "female-looking" crash-test dummies; even then, some were simply smaller versions of the male dummies and not anatomically, skeletally, or muscularly proportioned correctly.

This market oversight, not only bad for business because companies failed to address the needs of approximately half of their market population, also posed safety risks to their clients. Any drivers who were not "average" males — the elderly, the obese, the pregnant, even the short or tall — faced safety challenges and risked injury because of the way the safety features functioned relative to their specific physical needs.

Our tendency is to create products and services based on our personal experience. This is fine at the idea phase. But once you move into production, this narrow view can eliminate many potential clients who have needs your product does not address.

Cultivate Inclusivity in Your Offers and Your Business

If you have a reputation for inclusivity, how does that benefit your business?

When a visually impaired person experiences ease in your store (online or in person) do you think they may share that experience with others? Do you think that you would have an edge over competition because you make it easier for that group of customers to explore your offering?

When a car company builds a vehicle with a woman in mind, do you think she shares how comfortable she is in a car with her friends, her mother, her sister, and others? She may not even realize why she just feels more comfortable in this car — she doesn't have to stretch to change the heat, and the seatbelt doesn't cut against her neck — she just recognizes the car "fits" her.

Being inclusive is good for business in so many ways. Having a variety of viewpoints will help insure you look at your offer, marketing, product design and accessibility in a way that serves all your customers and potential customers.

Team

This brings us back to the people you bring into your business at every level. These are the people that will help provide their unique viewpoint if you allow and encourage sharing.

Intentionally seeking out individuals who differ from you — in culture, gender, experience, and skills — provides so many advantages. It may be extra work to reach beyond your current network, but this effort will pay dividends.

Not only does diversity and inclusion give you a depth to your product and service, but great financial benefits as well.

A 2019 study by McKinsey & Company[10] finds that companies in the top quartile for gender diversity on executive teams were 25% more likely to have above-average profitability than companies in the fourth quartile. The statistics for gender and cultural diversity across the entire company were equally compelling: the top quartile outperformed the fourth quartile by 36% in profitability.

Building a diverse team does not mean filling quotas or checking boxes on forms. For a diverse team to work, individuals must be valued for their differences and encouraged to share their thoughts to make the business, product, and service more comprehensive.

Inclusivity is a necessary companion to diversity. One cannot be fully realized without the other. When a person is an "only" in a room or group, they can doubt what they are feeling matters or that their ideas don't meet other's needs. But when each person in a room is an "other," feelings of "outsider" diminish and everyone's unique viewpoint can be recognized as valuable.

Being aware of your team's sensitivities is empathy in practice and it encourages better participation and expanded feedback. We discuss empathy more fully in chapter 7; it shows up here because we cannot practice diversity and inclusion without empathy. People must feel safe, valued, and encouraged to share their ideas and innovate freely.

The company that understands that embracing diversity allows capitalizing on a vast array of viewpoints will reap the benefits of those very views with comprehensive products and offerings serving a wide market.

Boundaries

Setting personal boundaries is another element to creating an inclusive community. It is feeling safe in a community that brings out the benefits of diversity, and this can only occur when people can set boundaries for their comfort.

Each person needs to be free to express their boundaries without fear of retribution, discussion, or quantifying. What one person feels is acceptable language or behavior might not be acceptable to another. Each person needs to respect the boundaries of others and feel free to both express and receive a boundary setting.

This may look like someone feeling free to say, "I do not read my work emails after 6pm on weekdays. Feel free to send me your email at any time, but please understand my response may be delayed based on my schedule. I will respond within X hours of receipt."

In that scenario, each person can continue the behavior that is comfortable for them and together they set expectations for how they will manage the boundary. If they need to create another level of communication for urgent matters, they'll continue the conversation to find a solution acceptable to both.

Boundaries are mostly about setting expectations — letting those around you know what is acceptable and comfortable for you and what is not. Most issues arise when someone crosses a boundary they may not have been aware of, or the person whose boundary was crossed doesn't feel comfortable holding their boundary.

By making clear in your business that personal boundaries are respected and practiced, the incidences of crossing will happen less. When boundary crossing does occur, a different conversation can happen; one embedded in the fabric of your business culture. Having this in place relieves shame or blame and builds a more cooperative environment.

When people feel respected by and in their environment, they are more invested in the team and dedicated to the company. A team that feels safe in their environment will bring more innovation to their work and their diversity will add depth to the company, product, or service.

Company Culture

The mission and values of your business are critical to building the culture of the company you develop. As the world is multi-cultural, -gender, -sexuality, and -racial (among other things), it would be shortsighted to limit your market through bias or unconscious oversight.

It serves you and your business well to build both diversity and inclusion into your company's mission from the outset.

Diversity and Inclusion Begins with You

Exploring your bias and personal experience is the first step to cultivating a more inclusive workplace. Surrounding yourself with other people who have experiences much different from your own will help round out your capabilities as a company, as a leader, and as a person.

As a business owner, your emotional intelligence will be the cornerstone of your efforts here. You have the responsibility and the privilege to create the culture of your company. By this one act, you take part in creating the world you wish to live in. Make your decisions intentionally and for the good of all, and you will be rewarded.

Bias and Diversity Exercises

Recognizing your own biases comes from examining how you see the world. Take time to:

- consider any stereotyping or typecasting in TV shows or movies you watch,

- recognize the stories different reporters are assigned to,

- take stock of the mix of individuals you regularly meet.

Consider the following to make diversity and inclusion a part of your company culture:

- Create inclusive language guidelines.

- Develop a vision or mission statement that defines the values of the company.

- Identify expectations for your team to communicate their boundaries.

Part 3

Withstanding the Inevitable Challenges

CHAPTER 10

Endurance

Success in life comes when you simply refuse to give up, with goals so strong that obstacles, failure, and loss only act as motivation.
– Unknown

In this chapter:
- Building resilience.
- Managing business phases.
- Roles for the entrepreneur.

Endurance is at the heart of success for most things in life. Outlasting the competition and working harder than anyone else has long been the advice sports coaches around the world provide.

In entrepreneurship we need more than brute strength. We need the mental fortitude to continue to pursue the goal long after the initial excitement has worn off. Maintaining conviction in the face of doubt and carrying your certainty in the face of uncertainty are just a few of the kinds of endurance you need to have a chance for success.

This cartoon is symbolic of what happens so often, in entrepreneurship and in life. Many entrepreneurs give up just as they were about to break through to what they had been working toward.

This is not just a meme; it happens all the time that the originally enthusiastic person runs out of steam, sometimes just before reaching their goal. Or the person believes they "should have reached" success by a certain point and walk away just before things would have turned for them. Or maybe the entrepreneur spent too much money in the initial stages and runs out of money just before they would have broken through.

We have all seen examples of seemingly overnight, raging successes in the world of business over the years. These examples give an incomplete view of how much goes on before that "overnight" success, or how to stay motivated during the climb — not only to reach success but also how to maintain it once you've "arrived."

I tell people all the time that an "overnight" success takes about ten years. Some take more and some take less time to become successful, but I use that number to help people understand that there is a lot to do to get to that point. You cannot just build an idea "and they will come;" it takes sustained effort, dedication, and endurance.

So if those stories of overnight success are not reality for most of us, how do we prepare ourselves for the long haul that might be our path to success? What type of endurance do entrepreneurs need to develop to get their products or services off the ground?

The Other R&R: Resilience & Resourcefulness

The difference between resilient and stable are
the way you come out of the storm.
–Simon Sinek

Resilience and resourcefulness are key ingredients in the initial stage of entrepreneurship. We have talked about the hard days that will come. But the days that are neither hard nor easy, depressing nor celebratory, that can be the toughest. It's the days or weeks when you just show up and do the thing, and no one is watching. Days when you think, "Is this thing on?" or "Is what I'm doing going to matter?"

You see, you expect the days that are hard; they give you something to push against. The days that are easy just seem to flow by. And the days that are celebratory seem like proof you are on the right track.

Building Resilience

Those days when you are just doing the work are critical. They are not very sexy or exciting, but they are plentiful. Having the resilience and tenacity to continue to show up day after day and put in the work to get the product built or the service marketable is where you make the magic happen — even though those days likely won't feel magical.

The key is doing the work that needs to be done while no one is really looking so that you can perform and deliver your best when the time to present comes. "Sweat more in training, bleed less in battle," as the saying goes.

The best way to build this endurance and tone this muscle is to schedule. I know, this is not sexy either, but it works. Schedule the work that needs to be done to move the business forward and make this a large part of your day. Always be sure to put in a little time for something that keeps you excited about your business. Don't worry about exactly what this "fun" thing is — but choose something that lights you up so you can maintain your peak performance on not-so-sexy stuff.

If you become drab about the work you're doing — just grinding it out to get it done and get on to the fun parts — your results will show that. Don't risk your end result with a lackluster mindset!

Cultivating Resourcefulness

Resourcefulness is a characteristic many entrepreneurs develop. Sometimes they overcome a challenge in their younger years, and sometimes they develop resourcefulness along their entrepreneurial journey.

If you are bootstrapping your company, resourcefulness is critical. You will need this skill to make ends meet until the money flows, and to stretch the money and resources you have.

If you are not bootstrapping, you will still need things outside your current reach and will need to find a way to obtain them. You might need to meet a contact who's just out of reach of your current network, or to acquire a tool or resource you know will be helpful but isn't in your current budget. You'll need to use your resourceful-ness to stretch what you have or reach for what you do not yet have.

As an entrepreneur you already likely think "outside the box" — resourcefulness is just an extension of this thinking. To have the mindset that there must be a way — or in the immortal words of Marie Forleo: "Everything is Figureoutable" — that's the basis of being resourceful.

This skill of resourcefulness is imperative as an entrepreneur and you can easily learn it if you don't possess it naturally. Shifting your mindset to one of certainty that everything has a solution is the best way to start.

This shift in mindset — knowing that there must be a way to do the thing you want to do — will automatically set you on a path. You may be amazed at how you see solutions appearing where you hadn't seen any before. Begin with framing questions in a way that sets your mind to solve them.

The best thing about the brain is that although it is an amazing machine, it doesn't know the difference between fact and fiction. So if you tell it one thing, it will go on a hunt to find and confirm it exists and is doable. When you tell your mind something is possible, you will prime the engine to get creative and locate or create the way.

So put your brain to work for you! There is always a way. Maybe you haven't done it before, maybe *no one* has done it before — but there is always a first and always a way. Once you know this to be true, you will find the person or thing you need to move forward.

This is not permission to step on or over people or get what you need at any expense. Only use this skill for good or you will damage your reputation and your business. This is not carte blanche to go out and grab what you need, it is a skill to fill needs creatively while building your products or services.

One of the beautiful things is that resourcefulness feeds resilience; the two go hand in hand. The more times you come across something unexpected or challenging, act resourcefully, and overcome the obstacles presented, the stronger your resilience grows.

This symbiotic relationship benefits you as the entrepreneur and plays a powerful role in your endurance throughout the journey.

Preparation

I find it no surprise that many entrepreneurs are also endurance or extreme athletes; many skills developed in one discipline cross over into the other. The first example is preparation. One simply doesn't wake up one day and decide to run a marathon. This is something a person decides, then plans, then executes on that plan — that's the way to run that distance.

Marathoners train in a way that they can build up to the full distance without hurting themselves. If they don't train properly, they might face an injury that keeps them from racing or going the full distance. There is no bigger disappointment for an athlete than having DNF (Did Not Finish) next to their name at the end of the competition.

The most important skill endurance athletes bring to entrepreneurship is their *dedication to the process*. Logging hours of training consistently is very much like the middle stages of entrepreneurship. Endurance athletes must train consistently to be ready for the challenges and build confidence in their ability to overcome them.

Showing up each day, whether it feels like you are getting closer to your goal or not, takes a bit of willpower and a lot of dedication. This is where the idea of focusing on the end goal has the most power.

If you are working towards something that you are not passionate about, the grind will become unbearable. If you thoroughly believe in what you are doing and what benefits it will provide to others, that passionate belief will help pull you through as long as you remain connected to it. The continual process of checking in and re-committing to the goal is a great way to maintain this energy.

Hang on for the Ride: Managing Energy and Interest

Fluctuations in your excitement level with your new project are inevitable, as Darren Hardy explains in his book *The Entrepreneur Rollercoaster: Why Now Is the Time to #JoinTheRide*. Preparing both intellectually and emotionally for the ups and downs will serve you well as the rollercoaster leaves the station and starts climbing that first big hill.

Entrepreneurship is not for the faint of heart. The emotional highs and lows can affect many entrepreneurs. Often the journey will take longer than you planned, both financially and physically. Be aware, plan for this, and stay the course, feeding your enthusiasm as you can.

Sometimes, we must define success as withstanding the journey and not giving up through the process. This "last person standing" model fuels the idea to "never quit" — since you fail only when you stop trying.

When asked about being an entrepreneur, Steve Jobs famously said, "It's really hard. And you have to do it over a sustained period of time. So if you don't love it, if you're not having fun doing it... you're going to give up. And that's what happens to most people, actually."

Motivational posters of the past — the ones that mockingly exhibit a climber reaching a snowy peak, along with the phrase "Don't ever give up!" — are unlikely to keep you as motivated as the intention. Reviewing your vision for your company and how the products or services you make will benefit others is a stronger method for moving through times when your excitement wanes. Fire up that passion and use it to fuel the work when challenges arise.

It is a tough balance for the entrepreneur to put in the work and energy into the project or business while maintaining themselves in peak performance. Keep in mind that your energy or excitement shift might be a sign of burnout. The earlier you recognize and address this, the better.

Determine what has brought about any change in excitement levels and address the issue, rather than just plowing through hoping it will change. The stage you are in might play a large part in this, but it is important to check in with yourself and make any needed changes.

Maintaining the energy of the human in charge of the company is a critical factor for a successful business. The good news is that there are many ways for you to generate energy to maintain your endurance through each phase.

If you feel your excitement about your project lessening or in jeopardy of cratering, a simple shift in physical energy might be the answer. Don't overlook moving your body and fueling it with good nutrients — even though we sometimes do this very thing when in the throes of building our businesses.

Tony Robbins — an entrepreneurial success story himself — consistently talks about changing physical states to create energy. This reminds me of Newton's first law of motion: an object in motion stays in motion. And while many have interpreted this as a confirmation of hustle mentality, the saying is much better applied as a call to activate a more energized, engaged, and creative state.

Steve Jobs is famous for taking meetings on a walk to bring a different energy to the event and potentially stir more creativity. Former President Obama and other previous presidents have also used moving meetings.

When we change the state of the body, from being seated all day or hunched over a computer screen, and add movement, that physiological change also creates changes in mood, mind, and focus. This is one way to add energy and help refresh ourselves.

The photos of desks littered with energy drinks and junk food wrappers strewn about are common from the days of the dot-coms. That era ended with stressed out, lonely people in bad health feeling like they did everything they could but failed. Unfortunately, they neglected the very things that would be with them regardless of the success of their business: themselves.

As I've said elsewhere in this book, it's critical to recognize that a human is behind every business. If the human cannot survive building the business, the price to build it might be too high. But only you can determine the price you're willing and able to pay in pursuit of your dreams.

I also want to emphasize that one does not need to sacrifice themselves to build an amazingly successful business. You can have a successful business and a full and fulfilling life at the same time — if you don't neglect one for the other.

The mindful act of *building the entrepreneur* at the same time or before the business is essential to both succeeding to their fullest.

All the time, effort and energy you put into knowing yourself and learning how different situations impact you will provide you with the skills to succeed in every area of your life.

Staying the Course

There are many things you can do on a tangible level to prepare as your business or service matures. Building your business with systems and processes from the very beginning will enable efficient scale and growth. If you didn't create these in the beginning, this stage is a great time to build them which should free up time for more creative opportunities.

As soon as the company begins to grow — even from one person to two — is the time to move some of the tasks that might be more mundane or less exciting for the entrepreneur to another person. Once you set up systems, you may even be able to contract tasks out if you are not ready for an employee. This process keeps you out of

the tasks and duties that sap your energy and time, and keep you more in the parts of the business that excite and feed you.

There is a lot of talk about the difference between *working in your business* and *working on your business*. This stage, when your business starts making significant progress, is when this mindset switch comes into play.

Working ON Your Business	Working IN Your Business
Creating Strategy	Implementing Strategy
Forecasting Market Evolution	Marketing Products or Services
Reviewing Industry Risks	Responding to Client Needs
Supporting Staff	Creating the Products & Services

Once you've created the structure of the product or service, your energy needs to shift from creation to maintaining and improving. Each activity has distinctly different needs and therefore the energy shift required can be tricky and hard to manage.

As the business develops, the needs of the company will change, and the entrepreneur will need to adjust. One must learn to read and adapt to the company's needs and be able to fulfill or hire for its continual growth.

Someone must be at the helm of the ship for it to stay on course, and it is critical to shift focus and potentially hand over the creator role to move into that of visionary leader. This role change takes courage, communication, and leadership to be effective.

Failure to anticipate this role shift, and to adjust accordingly, brings consequences. The climb is never all one terrain and as climbers, we must make modifications all along the ascent to handle the atmosphere and topography — all while maintaining the focus on the summit. Part of the complexity of endurance in entrepreneurship is recognizing, understanding, and training for the transformation at each stage of the journey.

Surviving Initial Success

The most complex stage the entrepreneur will face is initial success. Define success and what it means for your business as early in your journey as possible. Make sure this definition is yours and not society's or anyone else's. Be careful about being lulled into complacency in this phase.

Sara Blakely speaks openly about getting the first big purchase order for her now-billion-dollar company, Spanx. In countless interviews, she explains that getting the first order was only the beginning of her opportunities for success.

She details the extensive time she spent promoting sales in the very department stores that had ordered her product. Blakely identifies that her efforts *after* the initial order were the key to the success her company enjoys today.

Do not assume that because you know how amazing your product or service is that others will recognize the same. Do not be lured into the belief that someone else will be as passionate about promoting your work as you are.

Blakely became an evangelist of her brand to ensure others experienced her product. She didn't put it in the store and walk away thinking, "Okay, I've made it." Even Steve Jobs put on concert-like events to highlight and promote and build excitement for new products; he didn't just drop them into stores and run an ad campaign.

Take the time during your initial success to reach out to customers and show your enthusiasm and excitement for what you are bringing into the world. Ensure customers can experience and fall in love with your product or service and you will stand out from similar businesses.

Roles and Titles: Choosing the Best Fit

Entrepreneurs are most often the chief executives of their company, at least in the beginning stages. Early in a company's growth, the creator of the company holds both the company vision and a plan to drive that vision forward.

But the CEO of the company is not a tenure-track position; skill set should determine who fills that role. That means that the person who founded the company is not always the best person to run the company over the long term.

Self-awareness plays big here; especially when we must check our egos. The person who has an idea for a company may have the skills to create the visionary solution, to formulate a business around it, and even to produce the needed product or service — initially. And because of this, we often assume that this same person simply transitions from founder to CEO as the company grows.

But after the initial success of a company, the stages that follow present a completely different landscape and have different requirements. It is important for the entrepreneur to assess both their desires and talents to determine what role they want in the future and how it serves the company best. This needs to be a thoughtful decision, not an assumption.

For the entrepreneur to be the CEO of their company is not a requirement, and sometimes the company benefits when they are not. There are some who opt to continue creating; or some, like Steve Jobs, who choose to take the lead in one particular area and hire others to manage the other, high-level or daily company functions.

The difference between entrepreneur and CEO lies in a basket of soft skills. We have been led to believe those terms and roles are synonymous; they are not. Both have very distinctive skills required. A CEO drives the overall vision of the company and being the creator of the products or services is not (always) necessary.

This is where knowing yourself and your strengths and weaknesses is crucial. The person who thinks in big-picture terms may be unable to grasp all the day-to-day details needed to run a full company. This is also the place where the detail-oriented person may suffer from too tight a focus to move a company forward and may lack the strategic thinking necessary to maintain success in the marketplace.

Not all entrepreneurs have the skill, desire, or talent to run a company once they have created it. Traditional teachings about entrepreneurship often lack this key distinction, because of the assumption that owner and CEO must be the same. Self-awareness is your required skill here, to determine the best role for yourself over the life of your business and career.

Take advantage of this opportunity for forethought and develop the awareness and soft skills along the way to be aware enough and confident enough to hire for this position if the need arises.

Visionary

Sometimes a person is best suited to creating companies and visions and hiring others to bring those concepts forward. The knowledge of your strengths and overall self-awareness is important in this area.

Richard Branson is a prime example of a serial entrepreneur: one who has taken a vision and applied it repeatedly to different industries and companies. Some businesses have gone on to be amazingly successful and others have silently or famously closed in failure (Virgin Cola anyone?); but behind each of them is the same visionary creator — just with different executives to run each business.

Branson doesn't try to run each of his 400 companies as a CEO. which would be impossible for him to sustain and would not appropriately serve each company. Instead, he is the visionary. Through his oversight, each individual company under his umbrella maintains the Virgin brand, ideals, and principles, which dictate the framework by which the company operates in their unique indus try. On this large a scale, Branson has done this better than anyone I have seen.

Warren Buffett is another fantastic example of someone who is a visionary leader. He does not create companies himself but invests and acquires other companies regularly. Buffett is highly skilled at analyzing companies and recognizing where making changes can benefit the company's profitability. He oversees the vision but has no interest in stepping in and taking over the helm of any one company.

Although Buffett is not interested in being the CEO to any of the companies he acquires or invests in, his mindset brings broad-spectrum vision that enables improvements and benefits. The way a CEO runs a company is often one reason the company is attractive to Buffett. Another example of how self-awareness allows you to make the most of your talents.

People like Branson and Buffett can create an overall vision, communicate it, rally a group around it, and oversee its execution – all without being the CEO. These are examples of successful large-scale visionaries in today's market.

Similar visionaries (but at somewhat smaller scale) populate the hit TV show, *Shark Tank.* Many successful entrepreneurs on this show give their time, knowledge, and financing to bring others' products to market. They do not step into the CEO role, but instead lend their knowledge as a mentor and visionary.

When the Sharks invest in a company, they are not taking it over to run it. They already have many businesses of their own, just like Branson and Buffett. Instead, these serial entrepreneurs enjoy developing businesses and providing the visionary oversight to burgeoning businesses that are aligned with their area of expertise.

Many entrepreneurs today look to build a company in the anticipation of selling it. If the desire and skills you have are in envisioning and building new companies but ultimately not running them, then you may be a serial entrepreneur, and you are not required to remain the CEO.

You have options. Pursuing and finding the role that suits your talents, skills, and desire is up to you.

However, if you enjoy the leadership and the day-to-day running of a company, perhaps the CEO role is the right one for you.

Chief Executive Officer

A Chief Executive Officer is both a visionary and a company leader. Those who can inspire and lead a group of people to deliver on a vision and continually create, iterate, and pivot as necessary, make legendary CEOs.

A CEO needs to have the qualities to lead the company while creating a culture that drives development and innovation to move the company continually forward. For a company to have any lasting success, it must consistently anticipate and respond to the needs of its customers and the marketplace.

A skilled leader understands three things: the wants and needs of their customer base, their product/service and how it meets customer needs, and the talents and abilities of their team. This knowledge puts them in the perfect position to set the direction of the company by courageously and confidently anticipating the market and future needs of their customers.

CEO in the Maturing Company

As a company matures, the needs and the role of the CEO will also grow and change. The growth of the company is made possible only by the growth of the people who run it. A company can only grow as fast as the executive team's capabilities, and the CEO must direct, encourage, and support this mission with their insatiable curiosity, excitement, and example.

A successful CEO is a growth-minded person who understands that to keep the company relevant, they must continually learn, improve, and reach for the next level. This focus on continual learning and a culture of innovation will enable longevity for a company; the CEO has an integral role in both.

A CEO who cannot match his or her growth with the customer's needs will be unable to lead the company through turns in the economy, burst bubbles, and technology advances.

The world in which we live is growing and changing faster than ever, and the marketplace is progressing at an exponential rate. Those who cannot lead in such an environment put their company at a disadvantage.

A growth-oriented mindset may or may not be a natural gift, but we can develop it. To do so, we must tame our fear of failure and our perfectionism. Which brings us full circle to chapter 3: self-awareness is the most important skill for an entrepreneur.

Winning the Long Game

Entrepreneurship is a long-game and part of success is being able to stay "alive" long enough for people to discover and desire your products or services. Mentally prepare for the length of the journey, and you have a greater opportunity to reach your desired success.

Endurance Exercises

- Have you ever experienced a "flow state" or being "in the zone"? What types of activities have brought that on and how might you incorporate them into your routine?

- Where can you shift your attention from working IN your business to ON your business at your current stage?

- What is the ultimate role that you feel most compelled to fulfill in your business?

CHAPTER 11

Self-Care

In this chapter:
- Self-care for increased productivity.
- Choosing what works for you.

On April 6, 2007, Arianna Huffington, the co-founder of *The Huffington Post,* found herself on the floor in a pool of blood with a broken cheekbone. She would later learn that she had collapsed from simple exhaustion; no additional underlying medical condition caused the incident.

The eighteen-hour days she was spending building her business caught up to her and put her in grave danger. She credits this event and experience with changing the course of her life. No longer working eighteen-hour days, Huffington has built her new company, Thrive Global, dedicated to educating people on healthy work-life balance.

Stories like Huffington's are increasingly common, and yet so too is the pressure to hustle constantly. What hustle culture forgets is that as humans, we require care and maintenance. All of us do; do not fool yourself into thinking you are different.

Entrepreneurship is like parenting an infant, toddler, and teenager all at the same time. Excitement, stress, disappointment, discouragement, self-doubt, and celebration continuously interweave — and all in public view. This roller-coaster ride creates elation and nausea in equal measure, in no specific order, and without advance notice.

You might be inclined to skip this chapter altogether. You might have seen it in the table of contents and thought to yourself, "Eh, I don't need this fluff!"

I encourage you to spend the time now, or you may find yourself searching for this book later when you find yourself in a crisis.

Self-care is the fundamental preventative against stress and burnout. Like many things in life, the solution is simple, but often overlooked and seemingly in opposition to the nature of entrepreneurship.

There was a time, in this century, where people would call on the telephone to an office and if no one answered, they would call back later. As time and progress marched on, we hired assistants or voicemail to take messages for us when we were not available. Just a few decades ago, people expected to wait for responses. Now immediate response and attention are the expectation.

Technology has created the opportunity for people to be contacted at any time wherever they may be. While this technology has created great freedom for us to work from anywhere, at the same time it has shaped an expectation that we must respond immediately and be available constantly. That culture of hyper-availability, combined with the pressure to hustle every moment, feeds a culture of stress.

As of the writing of this book, the word "hustle" is the siren chant in the start-up and entrepreneurial worlds. This unhealthy attitude places personal needs behind business focus.

Hustle culture assumes a person can work an excessive number of hours (at least for a while) and this sacrifice for their business will eventually pay off. The underlying assumption is that "there will be time later" to focus on personal needs.

This mindset is not only harming our family lives and health, it's also detrimental to the productivity and business, especially when the business relies on the human affected. You cannot put off taking care of the person behind the business; if you are to continue to produce results, you must integrate self-care throughout the entire process.

It's not uncommon that I hear, "I'll sleep when I'm dead," and I admit, I've said these words myself, sometimes with great pride. I no longer say this myself, nor do I advocate this thinking for anyone else.

Article after article, book after book have been published about how important sleep is for clarity and productivity.

Just like the label on cigarette packages: the warning is clear but so many disregard the advice. We can create all kinds of excuses to disregard the warning, but the research is clear that burnout and physical depletion are the consistent result of the constant grind.

Obstacles to Caring for Yourself

What impedes self-care? There are many sources that drive the hustle mentality in the entrepreneurial world. They may have many derivatives, but the ultimate root is fear. This is where self-awareness is paramount to keep the fear in check.

Money is one of the biggest causes of stress and fear for entrepreneurs. Cash is an essential resource for the business to function, so cash flow is always top of mind. If investors are involved, their desire for a return on their investment, or to be paid back, adds even more pressure. Even governments, who question if a company has not identified a profit in a certain amount of time, can add another stress.

Scarcity thinking has a prominent place in this mentality. The idea that there are limited customers for any product or service is an exaggerated assumption that puts unnecessary stress on entrepreneurs. Very few industries have a customer base so small that this problem exists. Remember, there are billions of people on this planet!

The threat of competition also plays into scarcity fears. While a motivator for some entrepreneurs, obsession with your competition is a distraction that takes the focus off what you are creating and puts it onto another's product or service.

This is one of the most destructive and unproductive fears entrepreneurs can have and act on. Imagine running an entire race with your head turned so you can see your competition. How fast do you think you would run then? What obstacles in your own path would you miss? The same thing applies to the race of business, as well.

Another unproductive fear is the perceived need to get to market first in your industry (as we covered in chapter 6). Mostly ignored but proven time and time again: the first to market doesn't garner customer loyalty – the best in market does. The first to market needs to prove the necessity of a new product or service, while the best can wait and win in an awakened market. Contrary to popular belief, quality, not timing, creates market share.

As technology has allowed people to be available at all times, the fear that if we miss a call or contact, we miss an opportunity has fueled this tether to our phones. This fear of missing out (FOMO) developed in a society addicted to immediacy at the expense of productivity.

Some fears entrepreneurs face are real; some are simply perceived. The brain knows no difference between unfounded fears or actual threats and responds to both equally within the body. Understanding your fears and how you process them is critical for disarming them as they arise in your entrepreneurial journey. Just another example of self-awareness in practice.

Each of the fears above plays a role in our omission of self-care. They are the entrepreneurial fables that perpetuate the need for constant movement and the lack of focus on self-care.

No doubt you will work hard as an entrepreneur, but without self-care you will not work your best. The winner of the Indy 500 only performs at their peak because of their pit-stops. An athlete doesn't compete in an endurance competition without proper hydration or fuel. While entrepreneurship is not an official endurance sport, after all this you might wonder why it isn't.

Why Is Self-Care So Important?

One of the most important things for any human, let alone any entrepreneur, is their health and well-being. Focusing on something when you are not feeling well is difficult, and impossible if you are really sick. The best way to get the most out of yourself and everyone around you is to ensure your physical and mental health are at their prime.

The adage, "if you don't make time for your health today, you will need to make time for your illness tomorrow" exists because it is true. There is no glory in running yourself into the ground – and no guarantee that your business will benefit even if you do. Most likely, you and your business both will suffer.

To run a successful business, you must be in peak physical condition. If you are going to race the Indy 500, you are not going to bring a jalopy that has bald tires and needs an oil change. Your company deserves the same quality and dedication from its leader.

If you don't have your physical health, your focus on your business will suffer because you'll find yourself distracted by pain, discomfort, or illness symptoms and side effects. You'll have to direct much of your energy to overcoming those physical challenges, which limits the amount of energy and attention you can invest in running your business.

Productivity is another important reason to put effort into self-care. Putting more hours into the workday does not make people more productive. No matter what is at stake, rest periods and time off have been shown to increase both productivity and creativity.

Dr. Kevin Eschleman, an organizational psychologist for San Francisco State University, focuses on the psychological effects of creative, non-work activities. Eschleman's research clearly states that creative pursuits have a direct effect on factors such as problem-solving.[11] As an entrepreneur, this one of the prime functions of your role.

Risks of "Un-Self-Care": Burnout

Burnout is an inevitability without consistent self-care. Think of burnout like the "frog in the boiling water" story: heat begins slowly, almost imperceptibly to the frog, and eventually builds to a full boil. Avoid poaching your frog by reducing the heat or taking the pot off the stove.

A *Harvard Business Review* study on entrepreneurs and burnout levels revealed: 25% of entrepreneurs reported moderate levels, and 3% reported high levels.[12] Burnout not only diminishes work capacity and enjoyment, but it also diminishes the very characteristics that companies look for, like creativity and productivity.

Many people mistakenly believe they simply need to push through burnout. Those who think that if they just push a little harder and hustle a little more, they will get through to the other side and be okay, find out the hard way just how faulty this assumption is.

The challenge with burnout is this: the cure is to do less, often in the face of an ever-mounting need to do more. Pushing through this condition, instead of pausing to recharge, only drains our batteries more. As burnout sets in, productivity suffers, which feeds the stress and the desire to work harder to make up for the lost productivity — and soon we find ourselves caught in a vicious circle.

Applying self-care practices to incorporate a mix of work and rest is a challenge for many, but a necessary one for us to work (and live) our best. Getting this balance right enhances endurance and creates more enjoyment and productivity. It may feel strange to you to build in breaks and time off, but doing so will enhance your ability to contribute at your peak.

Stress Management

Your mental health is just as important to your business as the ideas and products themselves. Anything that puts a strain on the mental wellbeing of the entrepreneur will have consequences to the ability to give their strengths and creativity to the business.

Stress is common in the entrepreneurial lifestyle and learning to manage this pressure and weight is a critical skill to develop. Finding stress-management methods that work best for you will directly affect performance and, ultimately, your bottom line.

Along with everything else you need to focus on as an entrepreneur, you need to add in: sleep, exercise, healthy eating, stress management, and time for socialization. Piece of cake, right?

The beautiful thing about stress management is that there are so many products, services, and options to help you. I've listed several below as examples. Don't stress about your stress management! The aim is to try out one or two of these techniques to find what works best for you and incorporate them into your stress-management practice.

Meditation

You should sit in meditation for 20 minutes a day. Unless you're too busy, then you should sit for an hour.

–Zen Proverb

You don't have to go to an Ashram in India for a month to learn how to meditate, nor do you need to spend hours each day to get the benefits of a meditation practice. There are many different types of meditation and it makes sense to try a variety of types to find what works best for you. What I will emphatically tell you is that everyone can meditate. People will often tell me they can't, but I assure you they simply haven't found the technique that works for them.

Yoga

This is another practice that many feel gives them a place to disconnect from the busyness of life and simply quiet the pressures of the day. There are as many styles of yoga as there are meditation practices; simply find what you enjoy and get on the mat.

The many benefits of a regular yoga practice include lower blood pressure, improved sleep, and better concentration. Yoga also combats the sedentary lifestyle of most entrepreneurs. Again, this doesn't have to take up a lot of time in your week, but to know you have a space where you can disconnect and relax will reduce stress and improve creativity.

Journaling

This is an option for some of the more cerebral entrepreneurs. Many inventors and entrepreneurs and all presidents keep journals for many reasons. This is a great option to either empty your thoughts after a long day so you can rest better, to capture ideas when you wake and your mind is most creative, or as a record or a method for analyzing thoughts.

Regardless of how you use a journal, journaling is a useful method to clear your mind so you can focus. Choose the format that works best for you. I recommend physical writing over electronic; there is something about putting pen to paper that adds to the feeling of lightness and decompression. But find what works for you — format, time of day, and purpose.

Massage

Stress takes up residence in the body and can cause a multitude of problems. Muscles tense up and the continual presence of stress can affect the body's ability to relax over time.

Working tension out of the body through massage can improve circulation and energy, reduce pain, increase ease of sleep and raise your immunity. This may feel like a frivolous or selfish activity, but it has proven mental, physical, and psychological benefits especially for those under extreme or continual stress.

Professional Help

Talking to a therapist or counselor is another way to destress and decompress and work through challenges. Engaging someone whose sole purpose is to allow you to unload what is on your mind is freeing. And having an unbiased person, with no connection to your business or personal life, is invaluable.

Having a professional in your circle also releases your partner, spouse, family, and close friends from that role so they can be a source of support in a more intimate way.

Exercise

Exercise in any format is a great stress relief. There are more forms of exercise than I can mention here, but any form is a great option for maintaining both mental and physical health. As I've stated earlier, this doesn't have to take up tremendous amounts of time to be helpful; even 10 minutes of walking can be of benefit. Don't let a packed schedule stand in your way of getting on your feet.

The key to this is to find something that you truly enjoy. I worked for a former CEO and founder who played squash for a couple of lunch breaks each week at a local gym. He always came back with a renewed mood, and his productivity on those afternoons definitely improved.

It is amazing what a little movement will do for energy levels; it might seem counter intuitive — shouldn't we be tired after exercise? — but the opposite result is well documented.

Endurance and Extreme Athletes

Many CEOs and founders of startups are also extreme or endurance athletes. Many entrepreneurs compete in triathlons, are marathon (or more) runners, cyclists, and black-diamond skiers.

What is the connection between endurance/extreme athletics and entrepreneurs?

We can find some answers in the studies around flow. There is a large correlation between extreme athletics and the ability to enter a state of flow, a tremendously beneficial condition for entrepreneurs and athletes.

Some advantages of flow are now being studied and connected to increased work performance, creativity, and other benefits such as pattern recognition and correlation. Those who experience flow in one area of their life often have an easier time bringing it to other areas.

Richard Branson explained, "You have to get into the right frame of mind in order to perform your best, and need to be able to put setbacks behind you instantly. In effect, the discipline and determination it takes to compete as a professional athlete is not unlike what it takes to be an entrepreneur."[13]

Develop Your Own Self-Care Practices

Everyone has a plan until they get punched in the face.
–Mike Tyson

Stress that affects the entrepreneur ultimately affects the business. I have worked with several leaders that are great when things are going well, but change once stress levels increase. They communicate and make decisions differently, they may have short tempers, make rash decisions, or be unpleasant — all of which can be detrimental to the business.

Apply your skill of self-awareness to determine how stress affects you in these areas so you can prepare. Everything works together in the end to bring your best capabilities in the worst circumstances, but it all begins with awareness.

All of us need to have consistent practices to manage the volume of stress that comes with entrepreneurship. Although burnout or stress may not destroy you, it will have serious consequences — consequences which you can avoid. This is no fluff!

Self-care is the definitive antidote for stress, and the catalyst for gains in productivity, creativity, and problem solving. Maintain your human machine to its best capability and it will reward you with peak performance in its class.

Self-Care Exercises

- What's one area of self-care you consistently practice? How does it affect your day-to-day quality of life, and your ability in your business?

- What's one area of self-care you've enjoyed in the past? How could you bring that back into your routine?

- What's one area of self-care where you could use some improvement? Is there something you've never done (meditation, yoga, journaling) that you could try for a week?

CHAPTER 12

Ability to Ask for Help

Ask for help. Not because you are weak. But because you are strong.
–Les Brown

In this chapter:
- Strength training.
- Sources and methods of assistance.
- Lighten your load.

In a video interview recorded in 2011, Steve Jobs shared his perspective on asking for help. Jobs credits this trait as one that separates those who will become successful from those who won't:

> *I've never found anybody that didn't want to help me if I asked them for help... I called up Bill Hewlett when I was 12 years old. "Hi, I'm Steve Jobs. I'm 12 years old. I'm a student in high school. I want to build a frequency counter, and I was wondering if you have any spare parts I could have." He laughed, and he gave me the spare parts, and he gave me a job that summer at Hewlett-Packard... and I was in heaven.*

> *I've never found anyone who said no or hung up the phone when I called. I just asked. And when people ask me, I try to be responsive, to pay that debt of gratitude back.*

> *Most people never pick up the phone and call. Most people never ask, and that's what separates, sometimes, the people who do things from the people who just dream about them.*[14]

Why Asking for Help Is a Strength

Your ability to ask for help will save you time and energy, expand your resources, and make the difference between burnout and success.

Asking for help gives you a partner. It takes the moment when you are at capacity and brings additional ideas, energy — and possibly even an extra pair of hands — to the table. Your helper can provide resources, investigate options, brainstorm ideas, or iterate solutions that enable you to move forward faster and with more depth than if you walk that road alone.

Many entrepreneurs believe they need to build every aspect of their business as a solo pursuit. That is a huge mistake, because this belief limits you to only your own knowledge base, time allotment, and point of view. Without help or input from anyone else, you risk overlooking customer segments, solution sets, or opportunities to grow your business.

No matter your reasons for asking for help (or resisting it up to now), learn this necessary skill. No one reaches the top of the mountain alone. There will be many areas along the journey that require expertise that you do not currently have. Sure, you can learn what you don't know — but is that the best use of your time?

You'll gain no extra glory or benefit from isolating yourself — going it alone will only drain you and delay your progress.

I have worked as a paralegal for many years and have become well versed in sharing work with attorneys. Allowing a paralegal to work to their full capability saves the attorney time and allows the attorney to use their specialized knowledge to add value only they can, knowing the paralegal has covered the base needs.

An attorney can accomplish much more by engaging a paralegal. It's not that they cannot do the work themselves. But having someone else do some of the work allows the team to accomplish more in the same amount of time.

This time savings contributes directly to the bottom line, while allowing each person to add their unique value increases the overall value of the product or service.

As an entrepreneur, the same principle applies to you. You may quickly become overwhelmed (if you haven't already) with all the necessary tasks of running your business. And many of these necessary tasks will have a learning curve for you if you're planning to do them yourself. Yes, you can build your own website, but the work will likely take you twice as long and you'll end up with a poorer result than if you allow a web designer to do this task. Not only will you save time by employing another resource, but you can then focus on adding value where only you can.

Asking for help does not mean you abandon responsibility or oversight; it just alleviates some of the workload on projects outside your scope of talent and knowledge.

The entrepreneur oversees moving the vision forward, serving as the "talent" in whatever capacity the business needs, representing the company to investors and clients, and other responsibilities no one else in the company can do. Save your time and energy for the responsibilities that are uniquely yours, and that offer the most value to your customers and business.

Yes, you *could* do everything yourself, but there is little value in forcing yourself to do every item. You'll receive no extra merit badge for doing everything yourself — unless you count exhaustion and burnout as a badge — and I do not recommend that.

There are many approaches you can use to ask for help. Some assistance you will hire: either temporarily for a specific job or task, or as a more permanent team member. Other roles will be entirely outside of your day-to-day business operations (think experts/specialists like accountants and attorneys) but are no less important to the business.

The ability to recognize the need for, ask for, and accept help is one of your greatest strengths as a leader. Learn to do this well and not only will you benefit, but you will inspire those around you to do the same — which will improve your team and business by optimizing everyone's time, skills, and talents.

In the next sections I'll cover four sources of help that will serve you well in your entrepreneurial journey: mentors, coaches, and accountability groups and masterminds.

Mentors

A mentor is someone who sees more talent and ability within you than you see in yourself, and helps bring it out of you.
–Bob Proctor

One of the most important people you can add to your network is a mentor, or even better: many mentors. Mentors can shorten your learning time, alert you to potential pitfalls, and encourage you in ways that few others can.

A mentor will be a source of comfort, guidance, and accountability. They will be a sense of steadiness amid the uncertainty and often a voice of reason on the other end of the phone when you most need it. Because of their experience, they may have foresight that you would not.

Mentors may also connect their mentees with important contacts, which can reduce time initiating other helpful relationships. This is not to be expected however if introductions occur, it could save you years and nurturing those relationships is essential.

Don't miss the opportunity to accelerate your business journey by having a mentor in your corner. The most challenging part of the process is figuring out who and how.

Who Makes a Good Mentor?

Figuring out a good fit for a mentor is the first step. A mentor could be a former boss or teacher, friend, someone from your university or college, a professional group – or anyone who is ahead on the journey you are about to embark on. The standard advice is this: seek someone you would want to trade places with.

Richard Branson shares another approach in his story about creating Virgin Airlines. He reached out to Sir Fredie Laker, who had failed in the airline business years before. Branson explains that those who have failed can often give some of the best advice for your industry.

Someone from the same industry, whether or not they've been successful in that venture, will have background on potential complications and challenges specific to your market. Having a mentor from your industry is like having an experienced Sherpa to take you up a mountain. They have traveled the path before you and although each expedition is different, they know to look for, recognize, and navigate the hazards along the way. This guide will be a priceless addition to your team.

The Mentor-Mentee Relationship

For a mentor to be most helpful to you, you must be as honest with your mentor as you would be your doctor, which requires you both to establish trust. That strong bond of trust is critical, since this may be one of the few people who can support you at the critical steps of your journey.

But how do you establish this trust?

It is important that your mentor believes in you as a person even more than they believe in your business. The reason a mentor will take you under their wing is most often because they see promise in you. Any development your mentor provides you will last long beyond the business you are working on today, and they understand this even more than you might at this stage.

Mutual respect is also critical for the relationship to work. Although you are the one looking for guidance, the mentor respecting you is just as important. Both of you will put time and energy into this relationship and the investment in developing a mutual respect will grow over time and with your shared experiences.

Avoid an overbearing or condescending relationship at all costs. A good test is to ask yourself, "Would I invite this person over for dinner at my house?" You are not required to be friends, but having a mentor you enjoy spending time with is a must — or you may be hesitant to reach out when you need to.

Carefully consider several options who would be good mentors for you and reach out to them. If they cannot spare the time, do not take it personally. If you have set your sights on high-quality people, you may have to try many different people or wait until the timing is better for them. Keep this goal a priority because of the benefits it will bring you and your business.

Why Would Someone Be a Mentor?

Why do people choose to mentor the next generation of entrepreneurs? Many successful people desire to share their hard-won knowledge. Others want to pay forward the kindness and help provided to them as they were developing. There are as many reasons for choosing to become a mentor as there are mentors.

When successful entrepreneurs master business, or multiple businesses, they sometimes find the desire to help others becomes more important than creating yet another successful business. Those mentors seek other ways to add value and assist others in their journey.

Many mentors do not receive compensation for their time, although some do. Compensation or not, some type of reciprocation fuels the relationship and keeps the mentor interested and engaged.

Even though many mentors lend their time and expertise as of an act of service, do not take for granted the value of that resource. Time is a prized resource for all of us, and even more so for successful people. If they are willing to share their time with you, recognize the value, and compensate them in some way. Ask your mentor their reasons for helping you and ask how you might help them in return. Sometimes it is enough for the mentor to witness making a difference in someone else's life; be sure to always show your gratitude for the tremendous gift of their time and knowledge.

Coaches

Coaches fall somewhere between mentors and accountability groups. A business coach will help you develop goals and create a plan of the necessary steps to reach your ultimate objective.

While you receive input from mentors on what to expect and avoid, you plan your path with your coach. You work with them or a group to execute on the plan and review any unexpected items or results that appear along the way.

The full benefits of this role rely on transparency and honesty. Treat them as your business doctor. The coach can only be helpful if they have accurate information about your situation.

A good coach, combined with a good mentor, can help you maintain steady progress and assist you to reach your goals more efficiently.

Accountability Groups

An accountability group is a group of peers who gather on a regularly scheduled basis to help each other reach goals. This is a wonderful structure that helps each member stay on track with their stated goals and keep their promises (even those to themselves).

One benefit of an accountability group is that it encourages regular goal setting. The success rate for those who set regular goals and break them down into milestones is exponentially higher than for those who set goals infrequently (or not at all).

Your accomplishment rate increases when you add accountability to another person into the equation. Coupling regular goal setting with regular reporting to others about progress makes success much more attainable.

As a human, we are less likely to keep a promise to ourselves than to others. From experience, just the idea that I have stated to my accountability group I will do something cements that promise in a more prominent place in my mind and to-do list. The group's reciprocal nature is also important: as the group holds you to your actions, you hold them to theirs.

And while a mentor can hold you accountable, this is not the best use of your time with them. An accountability group can encourage you to action and help you reach the goals you have created with your mentor or coach.

An accountability group will help you make the most of your work with your mentor or coach by making sure you are continually taking actions required to move your business forward. Combining these methods of support will provide you the strongest possibility of success.

Masterminds

A specific type of accountability group is the *mastermind*. Mastermind groups are a concept developed by Napoleon Hill, author of popular self-help book *Think and Grow Rich*. Similar to an accountability group, a mastermind is where a group of peers, all at a similar stage of business, meet regularly to brainstorm solutions to business problems or share information relative to common business challenges. Accountability plays a part here, but a good mastermind offers other benefits as well.

Over time, your mastermind group develops an understanding of each member's business needs and goals. This special and unique relationship is an opportunity to give as much as we receive – a truly reciprocal affiliation.

My own mastermind saw talents in me I did not recognize in myself and recommended courses of action I had not considered. The group knew me, and my business, so well they could help me see opportunities I might not have taken action on without their encouragement.

Being part of a support group like a mastermind is an opportunity unlike any other, because group members are not involved in your business, yet they are emotionally invested in your success. The people in the group all face similar situations (but in different business phases, challenges, and even industries), which creates a large pool of ideas you can draw from. The group can encourage inspiration and help sustain momentum, both critical needs for the long entrepreneurial road.

This type of group is often easiest to reach out to when you feel a need – because you know you are giving as much benefit to the group as you are receiving, and because any challenge you are facing, the other members may be facing as well – or will be in the future.

Asking for Help Outside the Business

Becoming an entrepreneur will affect your entire life; it will engage your mind, your energy, your creativity, and much of your time. Finding ways to address tasks in your personal life is one way to create more time for your business (or for self-care — don't forget that!).

Maintaining your personal life is an area you may overlook when asking for help with your (new) lifestyle. Some things you may choose to forgo for a time, but you can't ignore or postpone the rest of your life while you build your business.

Consider paying others to pick up your dry cleaning, mow your lawn, walk your dog, and even bring groceries to your door — save yourself that time. Time is money in the world of entrepreneurship; paying another to do your errands is not a luxury, it is being smart with your time and energy. You can use the "extra" time to work on your business, to spend with other important people in your life, or for self-care.

Asking for help as an entrepreneur is a crucial step many overlook. Even those who started in their garage and dorm room asked for help — and because of the help they received, they were able to reach their dreams.

Ask for help to benefit from the experiences and wisdom of others, to collaborate and grow your business, and to save you time.

Make sure your circle contains a variety of people, to give you maximum support. And further, engage these people assets in the way that best serves you and them, so you don't inadvertently squander these precious resources.

As the saying goes: *if you want to go fast, go alone; if you want to go far, go together.*

Asking for Help Exercises

- Make a list of people who might be suitable candidates to mentor you and begin conversations with them.

- Research opportunities for entrepreneurial mastermind groups and attend a few meetings if possible.

- Identify every task you could delegate and begin off-loading the most time-consuming ones.

Ready for the Starting Line

Congratulations! You have completed your training.

The training you have just finished lets you put your best foot forward. You understand that operational knowledge, like training your body, is only part of the optimal performance equation, and so you have trained your mind also, in ways others don't realize is important or may believe is necessary. You know better.

Now the actual work begins: putting everything you've learned into practice. Where you apply your knowledge, assumptions, and drills. Where you refine your approaches and make "game-day" decisions. Where all your preparation meets exciting opportunity.

The tools and knowledge you have gained from this book are the equivalent of a course map in your hands. This map will allow you to predict and prepare for whatever lies ahead in your own entrepreneurial race.

You understand how to speak to the doubts and voices that will show up during the different parts of your journey. And best of all, you know when to expect them and how they may show up. You will not predict them all, but having worked some of them through will allow you to better handle those that arise unexpectedly.

Looking over the map again, you acknowledge the long road ahead, and you've prepared for the times when you'll feel like quitting. The road will challenge every drop of discipline your training created, but you know what works best for you to keep moving forward.

Every time you lace up you understand that only some results are in your control. Each course and event carries risks, many of which you can plan for. You know the methods that work best for you to manage them, which will save you time and angst and give you the best results.

Elizabeth Miner

You expect to encounter evaluation points throughout the course. You know hard decisions may arise and you have prepared to keep yourself in the best state to make the critical ones. Some tough calls are inevitable on the course, but you have a process to fit most circumstances.

You know that everyone on the course — from the registration table to the other competitors — are part of a whole that you belong to. Even in a competitive field, you benefit from understanding the people around you. In times of need, those people may be a lifeline, or you may be one for them. Battling for placement will take second thought to the personal connections you make — deeper and more important than the competition itself. These connections, you know, could make a critical difference at a difficult time.

You recognize that brute strength is not enough to propel you to the podium. You know that the rest days and time you allow yourself to absorb the training and experience have been equally important to your success. This feels somewhat counterintuitive to your drive but you know the risk of not taking care of yourself is a DNF — or worse, a career-ending injury.

To accomplish all that you wish in the timeframe and ease that is possible, you have learned you will need to engage others to help you. Reviewing the map, you see where you might stumble or need assistance. You identify those who can help and where to find them along your route. The aid stations are there not because you are weak, but because they can be the difference between limping along and curing an ailment for a stronger performance.

All along the course, you will put into practice what you have learned in this book. Some situations will play out exactly as you predicted and you will come prepared. Some will throw you a curve ball. But even then, you realize how much better equipped you are to handle challenging situations because of the work you've already done.

As you move along your entrepreneurial journey, you'll continue learning and practicing and improving. The core skills you have created — that powerful combination of emotional and operational knowledge — give you and your venture the best opportunity for success.

150

You didn't leave your training to chance. You have stepped up your game to prepare both mind and body to perform at your best.

You now have The Entrepreneur Advantage.

And when you come to the end of this race, you'll realize it is simply the beginning of the next one.

Acknowledgments

I've written in short form for years and had two children. Writing this book took longer and had more challenges – requiring a level of emotional intelligence that I, myself, had to expand!

I could not have produced this without the help of so many. Some will never know how much they helped and some are more obvious.

To my family, thank you for the countless hours listening, reading, and re-reading pieces of this book and giving feedback. I appreciate your support, encouragement, and faith that I had something to share from the talks and discussions we've had.

To my friends, both entrepreneurs and non-entrepreneurs, thank you for your encouragement even if you didn't understand sometimes how this all connected. I value that you were willing to tell me when things didn't make sense so that I could be more clear for this final version. I appreciate your patience with the conversations walking with me through doubts and fears to arrive in celebration of this completed project. I couldn't have done this without your support and encouragement!

To my steady, book confidant and editor, Steve, I thank you for your unwavering faith in me to get this out. I appreciate your guidance from the first coffee discussion to the moments of doubt through to the completion of this project. You have been my steadfast coach and reinforcement when I waivered or needed counsel.

To my team, both past and present, thank you for keeping everything rolling along as this project took longer and some unexpected turns throughout the process.

Thank you, Josh Nguyen, for creating our new home on the internet, ElizabethMiner.net, and being so willing to expand upon what you knew for all the elements I envisioned.

Thank you, Zachary Crooms, for bringing to life our content through your video prowess.

Thank you, Taylor Fisher, for your excitement, creativity and assistance on the early stages of book tour planning.

Thank you, Paola Sands, for creatively bringing our content to social media in an engaging way.

Thank you, Katie Dooley, for helping to bring form and function together through design elements that are often more felt than seen.

Thank you, Jeff Berman, for your creative counsel and support for this book and related forthcoming work.

To those I've met along the process of this book thank you for allowing me to start the conversation and play through theories with me. Your engagement and excitement about the concepts that landed on these pages are a result of countless conversations and experiences I have witnessed or you have shared.

To those of you that have gotten to this section in the book, I hope you continue to use this book as you move through your journey. Like any coaching, it is a continual practice. I hope you use this information to your advantage and I wish you great success in all that you pursue.

Elizabeth
MINER

Notes

1. Pressfield, Steven. 2002. *The War of Art: Break Through the Blocks and Win Your Inner Creative Battles*. Rugged Land Media, New York, NY.

2. Perlow, Leslie A., Hadley, Constance Noonan, and Eun, Eunice. 2017. "Stop the Meeting Madness, *Harvard Business Review* (July–August 2017): 62–69. https://hbr.org/2017/07/stop-the-meeting-madness

3. Branson, Richard. "What to Do When Things Go Wrong." Virgin.com. https://www.virgin.com/entrepreneur/richard-branson-what-dowhen-things-go-wrong

4. Wansink, Brian, and Sobal, Jeffery. 2007. "Mindless Eating: The 200 Daily Food Decisions We Overlook." *Environment and Behavior* 39 (January): 106-123. https://www.researchgate.net/publication/227344004_Mindless_Eating_The_200_Daily_Food_Decisions_We_Overlook

5. Danziger, Shai, Levav, Jonathan, and Avnaim-Pesso, Liora. 2011. "Extraneous factors in judicial decisions." *PNAS* 108 (17) 6889-6892; https://www.pnas.org/content/pnas/108/17/6889.full.pdf

6. Stark, Michael. 2012. "Obama's Way." *Vanity Fair*, October 2012. https://www.vanityfair.com/news/2012/10/michael-lewis-profile-barackobama

7. Patagonia Ad. *The New York Times*, November 25, 2011. https://www.patagonia.com/blog/wp-content/uploads/2016/07/nyt_11-25-11.pdf. Used with permission.

8. Schoemaker, Paul J. H., Krupp, Steve, and Howland, Samantha. 2013. "Strategic Leadership: The Essential Skills." *Harvard Business Review* (January–February 2013). https://hbr.org/2013/01/strategic-leadership-the-esssential-skills

9. Nobuo, Hayashi. 2019. "Delving into the minds of the heroes of the digital revolution." June 14, 2019. https://wisdom.nec.com/en/innovation/2019061201/index.html

10. Dixon-Fyle, Sundiatu, Dolan, Kevin, Hunt, Vivian, and Prince, Sara. 2020. "Diversity Wins; How Inclusion Matters." McKinsey & Company Report (May 19, 2020). https://www.mckinsey.com/featured-insights/diversity-and-inclusion/diversity-wins-how-inclusion-matters

11. Eschleman, Kevin J., Madsen, Jamie, Alarcon, Gene and Barelka, Alex. 2012. "Benefiting from creative activity: The positive relationships between creative activity, recovery experiences, and performance-related outcomes." *Journal of Occupational and Organizational Psychology* (April 17, 2014). http://www.eschleman.com/uploads/9/2/8/0/92800488/joop-2014-2.pdf

12. de Mol, Eva, Pollack, Jeff, and Ho, Violet T. 2018. "What Makes Entrepreneurs Burn Out." *Harvard Business Review* (updated April 10, 2018). https://hbr.org/2018/04/what-makes-entrepreneurs-burn-out

13. Branson, Richard. 2016. "Why Athletes Make Great Entrepreneurs." LinkedIn. August 17, 2016. https://www.linkedin.com/pulse/why-athletes-make-great-entrepreneurs-richard-branson/

14. Jobs, Steve. 1994. "Steve Jobs on Failure." Interview with the Santa Clara Valley Historical Association. https://youtu.be/zkTf0LmDqKI

E-Suite Membership

Welcome to the E-Suite; We Saved a Seat for You

When I think of CEOs and people that run companies, I think of what was once referred to as "Mahogany Row" or the "C-Suite."

This was the place with large offices and grand desks, leather furniture and big glass windows. This was where the big decisions got made and visions were drawn up for the company.

Today is different. People who run companies do it from coffee shops, kitchen tables, a desk in the spare room. It can be a lonely journey. There are times when having someone, or a community of people, who truly understand what you are dealing with would make all the difference.

The E-Suite is a space for entrepreneurs to be in community with others facing the same challenges. This is a place where you can come knowing what you say will be understood, where you can share your challenges with others facing similar hurdles. This is the space where you and your fellow entrepreneurs meet and support each other through tough times – collaborating, brainstorming, and sharing experiences, insights, and solutions.

Here you can deepen your emotional intelligence, your business, and your network. As much as you rely on your team or your partner, there is no one who will understand the challenges you face better than other entrepreneurs.

A community of creators

When people approach their business and lives from their deepest truth, they have a greater chance at success and happiness as a whole. The E-Suite is where entrepreneurs gather to learn, share resources and best practices, and confront challenges and opportunities together.

You don't have to do this alone. There is a whole community waiting to help you succeed today.

Join us in the E-Suite. https://the-e-suite.com

CPSIA information can be obtained
at www.ICGtesting.com
Printed in the USA
BVHW091141120921
616599BV00003B/4